Sustainable
Human Development

A young person's introduction

Based on the
United Nations Development Programme's
Human Development Reports
1990-2000

A project of Peace Child International

Project Co-ordinator:	David Woollcombe
Project Administrators:	Céline Schwob, Dominique Mansilla-Hermann, Heather Stabler
Final Editorial Team:	David Baines, Heather Stabler, Dhruv Malhotra, David Woollcombe
First Draft Design:	Caroline Dalcq
Second Draft Design	Francisco Pereira Moncayo
Third Draft and Final Design:	Jesús de Lasheras Andújar
Editor for Evans Brothers Limited:	Su Swallow
Project Supervision at UNDP:	Sarah Burd-Sharps
Project Consultants:	Caterina Ruggieri-Laderchi, Kate Raworth, Donovan Slack, Eirwen Harbottle
Educational Advisors:	John Burden, Mike New, Julian Cottendon, Tom Jolly, Carolyn Buxton, Steve Watts

Other Peace Child Publications include:
Rescue Mission Planet Earth - a children's version of Agenda 21
Pachamama - a young people's edition of UNEP's Global Environment Outlook
A World in Our Hands - a children's history of the past, present and future of the United Nations
Stand Up for Your Rights - a young people's book about human rights
Stand Up, Speak Out - a children's introduction to the Convention on the Rights of the Child
Be The Change! - youth solutions for the new millennium
Our Island, Your Island - an Agenda 21 for Cyprus
Peace Child 2000 - a musical play for children to explore issues of peace
Indicators for Action Pack - for young people to measure the sustainability of their community
Junior Indicators - a primary version of the Indicators for Action Pack

The concepts and measurement of Human Development as presented in this book are based on the Human Development Reports 1990-2000, an annual independent report commissioned by the United Nations Development Programme. (UNDP).
Peace Child International wishes to extend a special thanks to Dr Richard Jolly and Ms Sakiko Fukuda-Parr for dreaming up this project, and providing us with support, guidance and encouragement to enable us to complete it.
The production of this book was made possible by grants from the United Nations Development Programme and the John D. Rockefeller Foundation.

Printed in Hong Kong by Wing King Tong Co. Ltd. on chlorine-free paper from sustainably managed forests.
British Library Cataloguing in Publication Data.
1. Development Studies – Geography   Dewey Number: 333.1
ISBN: 0237523175
For further information and background study please refer to the UNDP Human Development Reports 1990-2000 [ISBN Nos: 0-19-506-481-X; 0-19-507147-6; 0-19-507773-3; 0-19-508457-8; 0-19-509170-1;0-19-510023-9; 0-19-510853-5; 0-19-511996-7; 0-19-512458-8; 0-19-513621-3; 0-19-521679-2] published by Oxford University Press; statistics drawn directly from the reports are referenced in the text, all other material is drawn from the young authors' own sources and thus cannot be verified as accurate by UNDP.

Sustainable Human Development

A young person's introduction

Based on the United Nations Development Programme's
Human Development Reports 1990-2000

Final Draft Editors
Chaffika Affaq - *Morocco*
Jimmy Allaire - *France*
Zuhra Bahman - *Afghanistan*
David Baines - *United Kingdom*
Roberta Benazzi - Marquez - *Brazil*
Tom Burke - *United Kingdom*
Dalal El Kortobi - *Morocco*
Ingrid Heindorf - *Germany*
Idir Kerkouche - *Algeria*
Dominique Mansilla-Hermann - *Argentina*
Juhi Nagarkatti - *India*
Denise Smith - *Canada*
Heather Stabler - *United Kingdom*
Veronika Stankova - *Czech Republic*

First Draft Editors
Mohammed Al-Abbas - *Jordan*
Melina D'Auria - *Argentina*
Dominique Mansilla-Hermann - *Argentina*
Marina Mansilla-Hermann - *Argentina*
Rob James - *USA*
Steven Apollo Kalule - *Uganda*
Astri Rahayi - *Indonesia*
Benedetta Rossi - *Italy*
Hanna Rådberg - *Sweden*
Hajara Kader Sani - *Niger*
Céline Schwob - *France*
Srijana Shrestha - *Nepal*
Pili Vicente - *Spain*

THE ROCKEFELLER
FOUNDATION

EVANS BROTHERS
LIMITED

U. N. D. P.

PEACE CHILD
INTERNATIONAL

Contents

Foreword

The challenge of human development is to provide every human being on the planet with a long, healthy and fulfilling life, free from poverty and full of opportunities to participate in the life of their community.

HUMAN DEVELOPMENT THINKING

Development thinking has been continually evolving since the end of the Second World War in 1945. Until ten years ago, however, the study, implementation and assessment of development focused too much on just one criterion of success: the national income per person. This is the amount of money a country earns in a year divided by the total number of its people - and it is fuelled by economic growth.

Income and growth are of course both central to the health of an economy but there is more to life than money – and there is more to development than economic success. In 1999, income per person in Saudi Arabia was US$ 10,800 and life expectancy was 71 years. Compare that to Sri Lanka where income per person was a mere US$ 3,300 but life expectancy was 72 years. Clearly, measuring income alone does not reveal all that we want to know about the state of people's lives.

Why not?

A visionary economist named Mahbub Ul Haq set out to answer this question. In 1989, with a small team of United Nations Development Programme (UNDP) colleagues and friends, he started the annual Human Development Reports (HDRs) which assess the success of nations in improving the well-being of their citizens. He and other thinkers created the Human Development Index, ranking countries according to how healthy and educated their citizens are, as well as their standard of living. The results are fascinating, especially when compared with GNP figures. As you read this book, you will learn about this and other measurements of human progress.

At the end of this book, you will be able to look up and compare some of the different national statistics collected on these development measurements by the Human Development Reports. These are just a very short summary of a much longer series of national statistics contained in the Reports each year.

Illustration by Hayato Kashimura, Japan

THE HUMAN DEVELOPMENT REPORTS

When the first HDRs were published, many of the ideas they contained were very new, and some were highly controversial. However, over the last decade, from the publication of the first Report in 1990 to the twelfth, which came out in 2001, major shifts have taken place in the approaches to promoting human progress and achievements. The Human Development Reports have contributed significantly to these shifts, from providing innovative analysis and powerful new tools for measuring human progress, to recommendations for new policies, to information which all citizens can use to challenge their governments about the condition of their lives.

For example, in Brazil the state of human development was calculated for over 5,000 local councils and ultimately brought about what was called the 'Robin Hood' law. Now the size and economic power of each council is not the only way in which the national budget is divided up between them. The new law calculates how much money each council should get depending on its level of human development and on concrete efforts to overcome poverty and inequality in these areas.

Similarly, after the launch of the HDR 1999 in Ireland, the government promised more funding to combat illiteracy in response to the discovery that over one-fifth of the population could not read well enough. These are just a couple of examples of how the HDRs have contributed to a shift towards more people-centred development.

PROMOTING HUMAN DEVELOPMENT

The Human Development Reports are prepared by a small, but dedicated, team at the Human Development Report Office (HDRO), but they are based on contributions from many others in UNDP and outside, including people from different countries all over the world. This book also shows how we all need to work together to promote human development - as individuals, as communities and, most importantly, as countries.

Barbara Ward, a pioneer of human development, passionately argued that, "the physical unity of our world has gone far ahead of our moral unity". Indeed, we can fly all around the world and make phone calls everywhere, but the gaps between rich and poor persist both within and between countries. Even now, 20 years after her death, the call she made for moral unity is too often neglected.

Today we have more resources, better technology and greater know-how for eradicating poverty than ever before. Yet still more than a hundred million children never get any formal schooling, and at least a billion people in poor countries lack access to clean water and basic health services.

Human development seeks to build people's capabilities and to broaden their choices so that they are able to live healthy, knowledgeable and satisfying lives. We hope you will be inspired by the ideas of human development and will be challenged to ask what human development means or could mean for you and your own community. We hope some of you may prepare a human development assessment of your own town, village or district, school, university or work-place. We also hope this book will be the start of a personal adventure, rewarding both for you and for others.

*Richard Jolly
Principal
Co-ordinator
Human Development
Report
(Photograph
courtesy of UNDP)*

*Sakiko Fukuda Parr
Director
Human Development
Report
(Photograph
courtesy of Maureen
Lynch/UNDP)*

*Mahbub Ul Haq
Founder
Human Development
Report
(Photograph
courtesy of UNDP)*

"Human security is not a concern with weapons. It is a concern with human dignity. In the last analysis, it is a child who did not die, a disease that did not spread, an ethnic tension that did not explode into war, a dissident who was not silenced, a human spirit that was not crushed."

Mahbub Ul Haq (1934-1998), Founder of the Human Development Report

Editors' Introduction

Human Development? What is that? It is about growth and development that produce happy people rather than lots of money. We have worked on the Human Development Reports for the last few months and we feel it is very important indeed, possibly the most important thing we have to learn in our whole lives.

Welcome to the world of human development!

Throughout history, people have dreamed of creating a world in which poverty no longer exists, in which there is health, education, clean water and shelter for all. Today, with our wealth and technology, it is easier to eradicate poverty than it has ever been. It would cost an additional US$40 billion a year in overseas development aid. This is much less than what Europeans spend on smoking every year; a tiny fraction of the money that flows through the world's money markets every day; and a twentieth of what we spend every year on weapons and the military; 0.16% of the world's total annual turnover. It is, in fact, a lot less than the total wealth of some of the world's richest individuals.

Even so, the world has not found this money or the will to eradicate poverty. Every day, over one billion people - one thousand million individuals - go to bed feeling hungry, and their 'bed' might be a street corner, doorway, or gutter. Most of you reading this will never have experienced poverty - the emptiness of feeling hungry and not knowing where to get food; the misery of being sick and not having a doctor to go to or medicines to take; the helplessness of feeling wet and cold and not having a home to go to. If you haven't lived like this then you cannot know what it is like, but maybe you can imagine. In our world today, where there are so many overweight, rich, wasteful people, over one thousand million people feel that way every day.

We can stop this and it is the job of our generation to learn how. We cannot turn all human beings into saints overnight but what we can do is to take people as they are. Most of us are good at heart; most of us want the best for ourselves and our planet and everyone who shares it with us. Therefore we can work to improve the situation for those billion people still living in poverty. What we also need to

remember is that it is in our own interests to do so because one billion poor could quickly grow to three or four billion poor in our lifetimes, posing a grave threat to the world's environmental support systems.

So, human development is not only about improving the lives of the world's poorest people. It is about saving our world and empowering everyone living in it as well. We think that this is a pretty important subject for young people to learn about. So turn the page and learn what we found out from the brilliant Human Development Reports.

Thanks.

When I was arguing that to help a one-meal-a-day family become a two-meal-a-day family, or that enabling a woman without a change of clothing to buy a second piece of clothing - that this is a development miracle, I was ridiculed! "That is not development!", I was reminded sternly, "Development is economic growth. Economic growth will bring everything". So we carried on our work as if we were engaged in some very undesirable activities. When UNDP's Human Development Reports came out we felt vindicated. We were no longer backstreet operators, we felt we were in the mainstream. Thanks, Human Development Reports.

Mohammed Yunus, Founder of the Grameen Bank

The Editors

It was a wonderful experience! A crazy bunch of people made our book grow from piles of pictures, essays and blank A3 pages into something great. We worked hard to make the book as fun and interesting as we could, and I only wish that I had had this kind of textbook. I'd definitely have learned more than I did from the dry textbook I had to use.

Juhi Nagarkatti, India

This book can provide you with information about the most important issues of human development. It is now up to you to actually do something about it.

Ingrid Heindorf, Germany

Human development is a strange and scientific term for 'human well-being'. However, it was only a short time ago that humans decided well-being was dependent upon factors other than money. Exploring this new vision of development with the editors changed my life forever. As you read this book, I hope that your life, and in turn, our world, will be similarly affected.

Donovan Slack, USA

It is up to each one of us to make a positive contribution to human development issues. Get educated, mobilised and empowered!

David Baines, UK

Writing a textbook for schools is a new challenge for Peace Child. This time young people are working to create something for their teachers in the classroom. I think this is a step forward for alternative education. I am very happy that the theme is human development. Enjoy this book and learn to become a responsible human in our amazing global village!

Dominique Mansilla Hermann, Argentina

Different nationalities, different backgrounds, different cultures, different colours, different clothes, different ages, different food, different music - but all with one aim: to write a different kind of text book!

Jimmy Allaire, France

I want teachers to use this book in a variety of new, innovative, dynamic, expressive ways to inspire young people to learn about development.

Tom Burke, England

The book is very good because now young people can learn all about human development and help change the future and make it better for them and their children.

Denise Smith, Canada

It was really hard work because there was so much fascinating information in the HDRs to fit in. However, for me at least, I feel we created something useful, interesting and inspiring.

Heather Stabler, England

I hope I've been that tool that will make the ideas of this book easier to read and understand - and if it inspires you to do something concrete from it, then I can say I've done my job well.

Caroline Dalcq, Belgium

It was difficult to condense ten years of Human Development Reports into a single text book. However, it is done and it won't take you as long to read as it took us to read the originals!

Chaffika Affaq, Morocco

I hope that this book will change young people's views and will play an important part in shaping their lives. It was hard work to put together and what kept me going was knowing that it was all true and very important information.

Roberta Marquez Benazzi, Brazil

As a Moroccan, I'm proud to participate in such an editorial meeting. It wasn't easy to put the whole book together. However, it was a great pleasure to achieve the wonderful harmony we had between the editors and to work with people from such different cultures and backgrounds.

Dalal El Kortobi, Morocco

Looking at the book I feel that it contains a lot about differences and inequalities. I hope that the people who read this book, instead of just feeling sympathy and compassion for other people, actually want to change things.

Zuhra Bahman, Afghanistan

1 Measuring Development

How To Measure Development

People are the real wealth of a nation. The basic objective of development is to create an enabling environment for people to enjoy long, healthy and creative lives. This may appear to be a simple truth but it is often forgotten in the immediate concern with the accumulation of commodities and financial wealth. (HDR 1990: p9)

THE HISTORY OF MEASURING DEVELOPMENT

Since the Second World War the most common measure of development has been economic income. This is measured through GNP (Gross National Product) or GDP (Gross Domestic Product). GNP is the total amount of money a country generates in a year, through goods produced, services provided and investments. GDP is very similar but it does not include any money which a country earns from outside sources, such as foreign companies. Both GNP and GDP are useful because they can be divided by the total number of people in a country to give income per capita (per person). The statistics for different countries can then be compared and analysed.

For many years the aim of most development was to boost a country's economic growth and consequently the average income per person. However, GNP and GDP do not give any indication as to the distribution of income within a country. For instance, in 1997 the GNP value of the United States was calculated at US$6,737 billion. With a population of 265 million people that would make average income per person US$25,423. However, there are many millionaires in the USA and millions of people doing menial or labouring jobs on very low incomes indeed. The average can therefore be a very misleading figure.

MEASURING HUMAN DEVELOPMENT TODAY

"Human Development is the process of enlarging people's choices - choices in relation to what they are able to do in their lives and in their communities" (HDR 1990: p10).

Development is about expanding the choices that people have so they can lead lives that they value. If people are to have choices in life then they need to have the capabilities to lead long and healthy lives, be knowledgeable and informed, and have the resources for a decent standard of living.

The first Human Development Report, in 1990, launched the Human Development Index (HDI) which is a very simple measure of these basic capabilities, combining:
- Life expectancy at birth
- Adult literacy and school enrolment rates
- Income per capita

Ten countries and their HDI rankings in 1998 (HDR 2000: pp157-160)					
	LIFE EXPECTANCY (YRS)	ADULT LITERACY RATE (%)	SCHOOL ENROLMENTS (%)	GDP PER CAPITA(US%$)	HDI RANKING
1. Canada	79.1	99.0	100	23,582	1
2. U.K	77.3	99.0	100	20,336	10
3. Poland	72.7	99.0	79	7,619	44
4. Cuba	75.8	96.4	73	3,967	56
5. Saudi Arabia	71.7	75.2	57	10,158	75
6. Sri Lanka	73.3	91.1	66	2,979	84
7. China	70.1	82.8	72	3,105	99
8. Pakistan	64.4	44.0	43	1,715	135
9. Mali	53.7	38.2	26	681	165
10.Chad	47.5	39.4	32	856	153

Canada - The Place To Be?

It is not only the HDR that has put Canada at the top of the HDI rankings as the best country for human development. A survey of 5,700 adults in 20 countries put Canada as the top place in the world to live.

However we, the youth, find things that worry us. The influence of the USA is threatening our unique Canadian heritage. The gap between rich and poor in our country is widening and nothing is being done to close it. Homelessness is a big problem. Canada has a reputation for compassion for the poor of other countries but in terms of looking after some of its own people, we feel it still has a long way to go.

Becky Carlin, 14, Canada

Every year the HDI ranks more than 170 countries according to these criteria. These rankings give a much broader assessment of development than income alone.

THE ISSUES

Of course the HDI doesn't include many other factors that affect people's well-being too, such as their working conditions, crime and insecurity, environmental pollution or a sense of community. Nor does it reveal how human development takes place. Are all people treated equally in the process? Do they have a say in setting the policies?

These and other important factors of human development are what will be explored in this book. For example, what can be done to manage the world's rapidly growing cities? Why is it so important for women to be empowered, both at home and at work? What is the impact of development on the environment? It is very important to understand that any policies that destroy our planet destroy our future.

Mali - A Place To Be Too!

The Minister of Culture from Mali, observing that Canada was at the top of the HDI table and her country was close to the bottom, is reported to have said:
"I have visited Canada and found many things to like about the country. Most of the people are well educated, healthy and have jobs which pay them more than enough money to survive and enjoy a high standard of living. However, I was also pleased to return to my own country as there is much about the Malian people - their culture and their traditions - that I find superior to Canada's. Our sense of community spirit is much stronger and people and families support each other and look after each other more. It is natural for us to look after each other's children and respect our old people but none of this is reflected in your HDI".

Look for indications of the level of development in this town.
An Urban Funeral by Madhurja Phukan, 15, India

QUESTIONS & ACTIVITIES *(Numbers in brackets indicate marks)*

1 a Put the life expectancy figures in rank order. Use an atlas to find out which continent each country is in. (3)

b What do your results show you about the global distribution of countries with the highest and lowest life expectancy figures? (2)

c Why is there such a variation in life expectancy between countries? (2)

d How can development help to increase life expectancy? (3)

2 a Draw a scattergraph to show the relationship between GDP per capita and the literacy rate.
What do the results show you about the relationship between income and literacy? (5)

b Look at your scattergraph. How useful is GDP per capita on its own as a measure of development? (2)

c Which country doesn't fit with the general pattern of your results? (1)

d Why do you think this is? (5)

What Is Poverty?

" Poverty is the absence of human development. It is the absence of individual choices and opportunities. It can prematurely shorten life. It can make life difficult, painful, even hazardous. It can deprive life of knowledge and communication, and it can rob life of dignity, confidence and self-respect - as well as the respect of others. (HDR 1997: p15) *"*

POVERTY MYTHS

There are many myths about poverty: that it exists only in poor, less economically developed countries; that it is a condition which people bring upon themselves; and that widespread poverty is not affected by our own actions. But poverty exists in every country in the world, including the wealthy and industrial nations. Poverty is a condition into which millions of people are born through no fault of their own, and in which many other millions of people find themselves as a result of political, economic and social events beyond their control. Poverty is influenced by everyday decisions which we all make, so an awareness of the issues is vitally important.

DEFINING POVERTY

In the same way that development has traditionally been defined as national income, so poverty has been seen as simply the lack of income. One common measure of poverty in less economically developed countries (LEDCs) is to count how many people live on less than $1 a day – that's just $365 a year. Today 1.2 billion people in LEDCs live on less than $1 a day.

If there is more to well-being than money, however, then there must be more to poverty than the lack of money. That is why the HDRs introduce the idea of human poverty which is being deprived of even the most basic capabilities: not leading a long and healthy life; not being knowledgeable; and not having the resources needed for a decent standard of living.

"Poverty is hunger, loneliness, nowhere to go when the day is over, deprivation, discrimination, abuse and illiteracy."
Single mother from Guyana

"Poverty is criminal because it does not allow people to be people. It is the cruellest denial of all of us human beings."
Educator from Colombia

"Wealth is the blanket we wear. Poverty is to have that blanket taken away."
NGO member from Botswana

Poverty
(from HDR 1997: p16-20)

"Poverty means never having quite enough to eat."
Beggar from the United States

"Poverty is the squatter mother whose hut has been torn down by the government for reasons she cannot understand."
Slum dweller from the Philippines

"Poverty is that impossibility of living in your own home. It is a life in a refugee camp and the loss of opportunity for my children."
Refugee from Azerbaijan

The Little Beggar

Her eyes are cold and empty. No smile on her lips;
If you ask her about happiness, she could not tell you
A word. She has never experienced anything like that.
Her mother makes her spend her life on the street.
She has resigned her life - nothing can touch her now.
But deep in her heart lies a dream - a village somewhere
Where she plays with brothers, sisters, friends,
Maybe goes to school, reads - but her eyes tell nothing.
We drop coins on her mat. Her expression changes not.

by Radka Pavelková, 22, Czech Republic

Photograph by Mandi Laziz, Algeria

MEASURING POVERTY

The Human Poverty Index (HPI) measures the proportion of people in a country who fall below a minimum levels in these capabilities. Even though human poverty exists in every country around the world, the way it is measured differs for more economically developed countries(MEDCs) and LEDCs. This is because there is a difference between absolute poverty and relative poverty. In LEDCs, many people live in absolute poverty because they fall below a minimum level. In MEDCs some people live in relative poverty because, though they may have more than the bare minimum, they still have very little compared to the rest of the people around them and this makes them both poor and excluded in their own society.

In LEDCs, human poverty is measured by the proportion of:
- Newborns not expected to reach age 40
- Adults who cannot read or write
- People with no access to clean water
- Children under five who are underweight.

In MEDCs, human poverty is measured by the proportion of:
- Newborns not expected to reach age 60
- Adults with poor reading and writing skills
- People living on a relatively low income
- Workers who are long-term unemployed

The HPI broadens the traditional understanding of poverty to include more than simply a low income. This is important as more money does not necessarily lead to more choices, better health or greater knowledge. Reducing poverty does not just involve increasing the income of the poorest people. It also means helping them use their existing resources and abilities to cope with the problems they face.

Money Isn't Everything!

Some people say that we cannot live without money and that money is the most important thing in the world. The more money we have the more things we can buy and the better education we can get. No wonder poor people can often only afford to send their children to primary school and not secondary school or university. How can they improve their life if they do not know how to do it? The next generation will also be poor. Lack of education is one of the biggest obstructions to overcoming poverty.

However, we can promote human development in other ways. People who have been educated can give other people lessons and the rich can help the poor by giving them food, clothes and other things. If everyone did this it might be possible to improve human development without money or a high income.

Anita Permatagari, Indonesia

Aspects of human poverty in LEDCs, 1998 (HDR 2000: pp169-171)				
	NEWBORNS NOT EXPECTED TO REACH 40 (%)	ADULT ILLITERACY RATE (%)	PEOPLE WITH NO ACCESS TO CLEAN WATER (%)	UNDERWEIGHT UNDER 5 YEAR OLDS (%)	HDI RANKING
Saudi Arabia	6	25	5	n/a	n/a
Bahrain	5	14	6	9	9
Cuba	5	4	7	9	3
Sri Lanka	5	9	43	34	35
China	8	17	33	16	30
Pakistan	14	56	21	38	68
Senegal	28	65	19	22	73
Mali	33	62	34	40	81
Chad	37	61	32	n/a	n/a

(n/a means not applicable or that the data was not available)

QUESTIONS & ACTIVITIES

1 What do you understand by the terms *absolute poverty* and *relative poverty*? (2)

2 Why is the Human Poverty Index (HPI) a better measure than just the lack of income. How is the HPI worked out? (6)

3 Group the countries in the table by region. What pattern do you see? Why do you think countries in Africa suffer so much poverty? What could be done to end it? (8)

4 Try to work out your own definition for poverty in your society. How would you measure it? (4)

Other Indicators Of Development

Indicators are tools which are used to measure different processes and situations. Indicators are important because they make it easy to compare large amounts of complex data on economic, social and environmental factors between communities or between nations over time.

WHAT ARE INDICATORS?

In a car or truck, the fuel gauge and the speedometer are 'indicators' which help you drive the vehicle. Global indicators of development such as the Human Development Index and the Human Poverty Index are indicators that help governments, and all of us, learn how to organise our planet better. By comparing indicators over time we can see what changes have taken place and understand the way in which our actions have influenced a particular place or situation. A great deal of work has been done developing accurate and reliable indicators on which policy and management decisions can be based. A summary of the HDR indicators from 1999 is included at the end of this book (see pages 80-86).

ECONOMIC INDICATORS

Indicators like Gross National Product (GNP) are used to assess the level of economic development of a country. Other economic indicators include the level of unemployment, the value of imported and exported goods and services, bank interest rates and the number of people involved in different industries. For many years economic indicators were seen as more important than social and environmental factors but the HDRs' emphasis on people and the environment has helped challenge this thinking.

SOCIAL INDICATORS

Social indicators of development measure how healthy and educated people are, by looking at the breakdown of their diet, levels of disease, and their life expectancy; or their

Illustration by Grupo Psimo, Argentina

..what would the indicators of human development be?

There are 52 women and 48 men: 57 Asians, 21 Europeans, 8 Africans and 14 from the Americas. Only 30 are white. 89 are heterosexual. 15 of the inhabitants live in an affluent area of the village and about 78 in poorer districts. The other 7 live in a neighbourhood that is partially developed.

The average income per person is $6,000 a year, but in reality nearly half of the inhabitants survive on less than $2 per day. 22 villagers, two thirds of whom are women, are illiterate. Of the 39 people under 20 years of age, 75% live in poorer districts and many of them are looking for jobs that do not exist.

Six people own a computer but only two of them have access to the Internet. More than half the population of the village have never made or received a telephone call.

In the affluent district, people live for nearly 78 years; in poorer areas 64 years and in the poorest neighbourhoods only 52 years. Infectious diseases, malnutrition and a lack of access to safe water, sanitation, health care, adequate housing, education and work all combine to create a higher incidence of fatal diseases to create harsher conditions and shorter life spans in the poor districts.

Naysun Alae-Carew, 14, Scotland
(with some help from The Millennium Report by Kofi Annan, Secretary General of the United Nations)

A COST-BENEFIT ANALYSIS OF BUILDING A BYPASS AROUND A TOWN

One way of using indicators is in a cost-benefit analysis. This compares what something costs with the benefits that it brings and helps people make decisions about the best course of action. A full cost benefit analysis includes social, environmental and economic factors. Sometimes you can put a number on all the costs and the benefits but this is not always possible and you have to make a decision based on the community's instincts and values.

Costs

- Economic
  Building the road
  Buying the land
- Social
  Loss of arable land
  Breakup of rural communities
- Environmental
  Damage to ecological habitats
  Lost beauty and peace in the countryside

Benefits

- Economic
  Shorter journey times so less petrol costs
  Encourages more businesses
- Social
  Less traffic in town
  Safer shopping areas
- Environmental
  Enhanced tranquillity, better quality of life in town
  Better air quality in town

---

access to services and amenities such as clean water, sanitation, doctors and schools.

UNICEF, the United Nation's Children's Fund, uses indicators based on death rates. The infant mortality rate (IMR) is the number of children per thousand who die within a year of being born. The child mortality rate, also called the under five mortality rate (U5MR), is the number of children per thousand who die before their fifth birthday. The U5MR figures are revealing because if children live beyond the age of five it implies that they had adequate nutrition, access to primary health care, and that their mother probably had a basic education and pre-natal care. These all indicate a basic standard of human development.

ENVIRONMENTAL INDICATORS

Environmental indicators involve monitoring things such as air, water and land pollution, as well as the bio-diversity of a particular area. The use of such indicators has increased understanding of the wider environmental impact of individual and corporate decisions and activities. 'Full-cost accounting' or 'green accounting' includes an awareness of the effect on the environment of development projects. Natural resources such as primary forests or clean coastlines are given an ecological value as well as an economic one.

Economic and social indicators of development (HDR 1997: pp137-231)			
	AGRICULTURE AS % OF GDP (1997)	TVS PER 100 PEOPLE (1996)	U5MR AS % (1997)
1. Canada	n/a	71	7
2. United Kingdom	2	61	7
3. Saudi Arabia	n/a	42	11
4. Poland	n/a	20	8
5. Cuba	6	26	28
6. Sri Lanka	22	8	19
7. China	19	25	47
8. Pakistan	25	2	136
9. Chad	49	1	239
10. Mali	39	0.2	198

(n/a means not applicable or that the data was not available)

QUESTIONS & ACTIVITIES

1. Why are IMR and U5MR both useful indicators of levels of development? (2)
2. What is green accounting and in what ways does it influence a cost-benefit analysis? (3)
3. Study a local development issue, such as the building of a new road or retail outlet.
   a. Complete a cost-benefit for the development.
   b. Produce an annotated sketch map of the development, adding labels to indicate both positive and negative outcomes as a result of the development.
   c. Looking at your results, would you allow the development to go ahead? Imagine you are a local newspaper reporter at a public meeting to discuss the development. Write a short article reporting who said what and what issues were raised. (10)

2 Our Divided World

Describing The Divisions

Some say our world is a global village - but the divisions between rich and poor, between those with opportunity and those without, are dramatic. These divisions don't just exist within our world, but also within countries and even within cities.

NO SIMPLE DESCRIPTION

There are many ways to describe the economic, political, social and cultural divisions in our world: rich/poor, North/South, East/West, First World/ Third World, developed/developing, industrialised/ non-industrialised.

Today the preferred terms are More Economically Developed Countries (MEDCs) and Less Economically Developed Countries (LEDCs). These terms have been chosen because no country is fully developed as yet; not all LEDCs are in the south

and many of them are industrialised; and the concept of First and Third Worlds suggests a system of ranking that is not appropriate. Each and every country still faces a number of challenges when promoting human development for all its citizens.

Case Study

BRAZIL
Capital: Brazilia
Area: 8,511,965 sq km
Population: 163,700,000

Social Inequality In Brazil

Society in Brazil is far from equal. Social inequality is amongst the worst in the world. This absurd inequality brings terrible consequences to the entire society. It causes social exclusion and very high crime rates. Crime becomes a 'solution' for those who don't have enough food or clothes.

In Brazil it is possible to find large mansions with the most efficient security systems, guards and guard dogs, whilst out on the streets there are beggars who don't know when it will be possible to have their next meal. Since the rich have more influence over the government, they have the power to make this situation permanent, and they do.

The only hope poor people have to change their lives is education. They need skills to find employment. They need exams to get qualifications. Some of them might reach university and get a degree, but this is very hard for the poorest, as they can not afford the school fees. They are stuck with nowhere to go. However, I know this situation is not unique to Brazil and that similar inequalities exist in many countries around the world.

Roberta Benazzi Marquez, 16, Brazil

The 'Champagne Glass' depiction of the gap between rich and poor (1992 HDR, front cover).
The top of the glass represents the richest 20% of the world's population which receives 82.7% of the total world income and uses the majority of its resources. The bottom of the glass represents the poorest 20% of the world's population which receives only 1.4% of the world's income and consumes very little of its resources.

Illustration by Marielle Smith, 17, UK

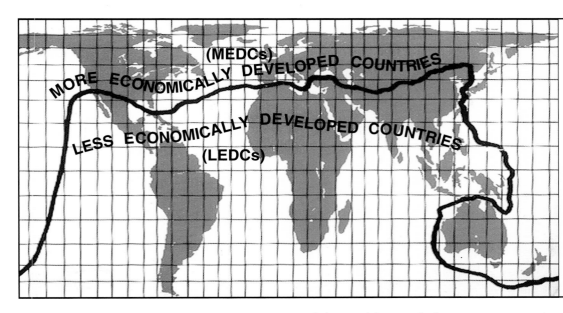

Rethinking The North-South Divide

(From North-South: A Programme For Survival, 1980)

The line separates the wealthier, more industrialised MEDCs from the poorer and less industrialised LEDCs. However, since the breakdown of communist regimes in the late 1980s, a number of countries in Central and Eastern Europe, classed as MEDCs, are experiencing severe poverty levels like those found in LEDCs.

THE INEQUALITY GAP

Inequalities in wealth

● The combined wealth of the 225 richest people in the world is equal to that of the poorest half of the world's population.

● The combined wealth of the world's 15 richest people is more than the total income of all sub-Saharan African countries.

● 4% of the combined wealth of the world's 225 richest people would feed, clothe and shelter all the world's poorest people.

These divisions are not just economic. There are lots of inequalities:

Inequalities in trade

● The poorest 20% of the world's population control only 1% of world trade.

● The poorest 20% of the world's population receives only 0.2% of bank loans.

● The poorest 20% of the world's population receives only 0.2% of Foreign Direct Investment (money invested by foreign governments or companies).

Inequalities in education and technology

● Less than 2% of people in LEDCs go to university compared with 37% in MEDCs.

● 80% of the world's people live in LEDCs, but only 4% of the world's academic, technological or scientific research is done there.

● Scientific and technical employees number 81 per thousand in MEDCs but only 9 per thousand in LEDCs.

Inequalities in consumption

● The top 25% of the world's population consumes about 70% of the world's energy, 75% of its metals, 85% of its wood and 60% of its food.

REINFORCING THE GAP

The problem with such inequalities between countries is that they tend to reinforce each other. Unequal incomes mean unequal opportunities for governments to provide education and fund science research. That leads to inequalities in countries' abilities to create new technologies to solve their own problems and raise worker productivity – and that feeds back into inequalities in the income they generate. Inequality creates a vicious circle.

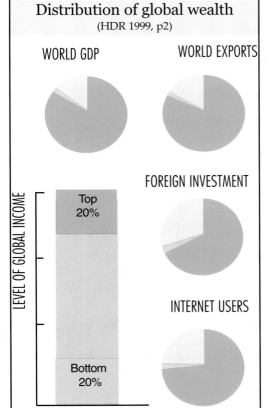

Distribution of global wealth
(HDR 1999, p2)

QUESTIONS & ACTIVITIES

1 Why are the terms MEDCs and LEDCs now used to describe the divisions in our world rather than other terms? (2)

2 Explain some of the reasons why the gap between the haves and the have-nots is so wide. Use specific answers from the information on this page to illustrate your answer. (4)

3 Is the North-South divide an accurate representation of the divisions in the world today? Give reasons for your answer. (4)

4 Make a list of the MEDCs and LEDCs. What patterns do you see among the continents? (5)

Contrasts In Experience

Although the Czech Republic and Japan are both defined as MEDCs there are big differences between them. Japan ended the 20th century with $24,900 per capita income whilst the Czech Republic had only $13,000. The two countries had very different political structures and economic policies which affected their level of human development.

CZECH REPUBLIC	
Capital: Prague	
Area: 78,864 sq km	
Population: 10,346,000	
Currency: Koruna/Crown	

JAPAN	
Capital: Tokyo	
Area: 377,835 sq km	
Population: 125,362,000	
Currency: Yen	

ECONOMIC POLICY

Before the Second World War Czechoslovakia was one of Europe's leading industrial powers. However, after the war the Soviet Union occupied Czechoslovakia, taking all the products and profits of its industry without investing in new technologies. The Soviets also imposed a communist regime on Czechoslovakia. All industries and services were owned and managed by the state, not always very efficiently or safely, and there were strict controls over people's social and political freedom. In 1989 the country became independent from the Soviet Union and in 1993 divided into the Czech Republic and Slovakia.

This was in sharp contrast to Japanese economic policy. The United States' occupation of Japan ended in 1955, and since then the Ministry of International Trade & Industry(MITI) has invested heavily in the latest technologies and production techniques offering the most potential for growth and profit. For example, Japan has become a major steel exporter even though it has to import all the iron ore and coal actually needed to produce it.

The Czech Republic has a large supply of raw materials on which to base its development, but formerly lacked the organisational, management and investment policies of Japan.

"Japan's astonishing economic ascendancy has been based on a combination of good economic management and decisive investment in human capital. With 3% of the world's land area and 2.3% of the population, it contributes 16% to the world economy." (HDR 1992: p72).

HUMAN DEVELOPMENT POLICIES

Good economic policies are essential for human development, but social and environmental policies are equally important. Since independence, the Czech Republic has worked hard to improve the living and working conditions of its citizens by promoting education, health and gender equality.

"The Czech Republic, along with Hungary and Poland, was an early starter in the economic, social and political transformation to a market economy. There was also a psychological transformation created by the arrival of freedom of travel, freedom of expression and the change from a life in which the state provided everything to one where living standards depend on private initiative and effort" (HDR 1993: p44).

At the heart of Japan's economic success lies a strong emphasis on education. The social status of teachers in

A motor manufacturer in the Czech Republic. During the communist era it was run by the state but now it is privately owned.

Photograph by Blanka Tomancaková 25, Czech Republic

Japan is one of the world's most industrialised countries and one of the top ten countries in the HDI rankings.

Photograph by Mathias Fiegle, www.lomo.com

HDI evolving over 25 years in Japan, the Czech Republic and the United Kingdom.

(HDR 2000: p145)

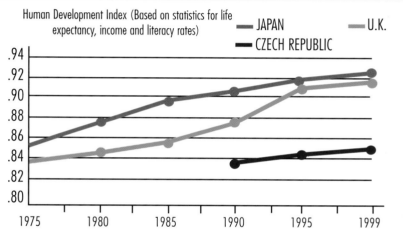

Human Development Index (Based on statistics for life expectancy, income and literacy rates)

— JAPAN — U.K. — CZECH REPUBLIC

Japan is very high and Japan spends $2,208 per capita on education – six and a half times the world average of $336. This investment in education has been incredibly successful, and today 90% of Japanese managers have university degrees.

In Japan, wages have risen recently, and the gap between rich and poor has shrunk. For 40 years, unemployment was under 3%, one of the lowest rates in the world. Also, Japanese companies take care of their workers, often providing them with all

kinds of medical and leisure benefits, and retraining them for new jobs rather than hiring new people. Despite the pressures of education and work, people in Japan work hard and play hard, and Japanese society is still an excellent example of investment in people and successful human development.

Life Before And After Communism

During the communist regime foreign goods were only available sometimes, like over Christmas. You had to wait many hours in a queue and sometimes, when you got to the end of it, you could not buy anything. There was never any tropical fruit, no nice clothes, no cosmetics, kitchen tools – nothing!

It was not because there was poverty, it was just that the communists did not allow imports. You could only buy goods manufactured in the Czech Republic or other communist countries. There was a network of 'Tuzex' shops, where you could buy high quality goods with foreign currency, but they were very expensive. Some people did travel abroad and could see what we were missing. After the "Velvet Revolution" of 1989, when we finally achieved independence, democracy came, along with no restrictions on travel, free speech, and freedom to import whatever you wanted. I believe that no one would want the old days to come back. These new freedoms are more important to us than anything that money can buy.

Veronika Stanikova, 15, Czech Republic

QUESTIONS & ACTIVITIES

1 a What were the HDI values of the Czech Republic and Japan in 1999? (2)

  b Why do you think there are no data for the Czech Republic before 1990? (2)

2 Draw up a table comparing the economic development of the Czech Republic and Japan since the Second World War. Use headings like political systems, education, wages and care of workers. (6)

3 Use books, or the Internet if you have access to it, to find out about the imports and exports of the Czech Republic and Japan. What do your results tell you about the economy and employment in each country? (6)

Internal Differences

The UK and India have historically had strong hierarchies where groups of people are ranked and treated differently according to their social and economic background. In the UK it is called the class system and in India it is called the caste system. These internal divisions mean that not everyone shares the same level of human development.

UNITED KINGDOM
Capital: London
Area: 244,177 sq km
Population: 58,258,000

INDIA
Capital: New Delhi
Area: 3,287,263 sq km
Population: 935,744,000

UNITED KINGDOM

Despite its history as one of the world's biggest empires, and the economic boom of the 1980s, the UK has some of the worst poverty among MEDCs. The HDRs have drawn attention to the rise of a large number of people living in poverty in the UK.

● The income share of the richest 20% of the population is ten times as much as the poorest 20%.

● The number of families living below the poverty line rose 60% between 1978 & 1990.

● Over half the children in single-parent families live below the poverty line.

● 1.5 million people cannot afford an adequate diet for minimum levels of health.

● The rich keep getting richer. Incomes of the richest 20% rose 2.2% in the 1980s. For the poorest, they rose by just 0.3%.

U.K	HDR 1999	India
NO. 10	HDI PLACEMENT	NO. 132
POUND STERLING	CURRENCY UNIT	INDIAN RUPEE
1,231.3 BILLION	GNP - 1997 (IN US$)	357.4 BILLION
20,870	GNP PER CAPITA -1995 (US$)	370
77.2 YEARS	LIFE EXPECTANCY AT BIRTH	62.6 YEARS
164	DOCTORS (PER 100,000 PEOPLE -1993)	48
6	INFANT MORTALITY RATE PER 1000 LIVE BIRTHS (1997)	71
9	MATERNAL MORTALITY RATE PER 100,000 LIVE BIRTHS (1990)	570
6.9%	WOMEN IN ALL LEVELS OF GOVERNMENT	5.8%
	NET ENROLMENT RATIO IN SCHOOL (AS % OF RELEVANT AGE GROUP - 1997):	
99.9%	PRIMARY SCHOOL	77.2%
91.8%	SECONDARY SCHOOL	59.7%
	ADULT LITERACY RATE % IN 1997:	
99.0%	FEMALE	39.4%
99.0%	MALE	66.7%

INDIA

India has a very large and diverse population of over a billion people. There are fourteen official languages and over one thousand local dialects. The HDRs highlight the big differences between the regional ethnic groups and members of different castes.

● In a South Indian village the literacy rate in 1989 was 90% for the Brahmins (high caste) and 10% for people at the lower end of the caste hierarchy.

● In India literacy among the general population is 52% but among the communities classified as low caste it is only 30%.

● In rural Punjab child mortality among the landless is 36% higher than among the land-owning classes.

● Life expectancy in the state of Kerala is 72 years but only 54 years in the state of Madhya Pradesh.

Homelessness is a serious problem in the UK.

Photograph by Tom Jolly, UK

Poverty In The UK

Poverty doesn't just exist in a far-off foreign land. It's not just people on the TV news or in an Oxfam advert who are poor. They also live here in the UK. It is estimated that 24% of the population, 13.6 million people, are living in poverty in the UK, allegedly one of the most developed countries in the world.

Poverty in the UK is about social exclusion imposed by an inadequate income. It's about not having enough money to send children on school trips. It's about dreading Christmas because you cannot afford presents. It's about not having the occasional treat and not being able to buy new clothes.

I live in Plymouth, a relatively large city in south-west England. There are huge inequalities in the city. Some people live in large houses, with large gardens, with a digital TV in every bedroom. They wear their designer clothes and spend their time deciding where to go on holiday each year, Florida or Barbados?

Other people live in dilapidated, small council flats, wondering how they can make their social security payment last that little bit longer. How will they afford a new school uniform when their son joins secondary school if they cannot afford food?

I think that poverty is a disgrace on UK society and it should be an urgent priority to eradicate it. This is not just about giving people jobs - many jobs are low-skilled, low paid, insecure part-time temporary work. In order to achieve a sustainable, developed society in the UK we also have to address education, social security, housing and social attitudes. This is a big challenge.

Tom Burke, 16, Plymouth

Inequalities In India

Today India is a world leader in computer technology as well as scientific research and educational institutions. It is almost self-sufficient in food production, has a very efficient postal system and one of the largest fully functional rail networks in the world. India's diverse communities and ethnic races all enjoy equal political representation, and special places are reserved in education, jobs and governance for religious and social minorities.

However, there are still problems and divisions between groups. The caste system still exists and religious intolerance is at its highest level. Marriage partners are often carefully screened and chosen by the parents and a match is made to maintain the 'purity' of caste. Marriages of choice can be severely frowned upon. In some cases this has even led to the disowning of children and families breaking up. Local politics are nearly always governed by high castes and there is a lot of favouritism where jobs and services are given to friends and relatives before other people.

The country is overburdened with a huge, corrupt and inefficient bureaucracy. The education and economic policies do not do enough to help the people who are most disadvantaged - women, children and the very poor.

Rural communities that form the backbone of India's agricultural economy are for the most part ignored, except at election time, and, as a result, lack social welfare benefits and basic health services. Even where such facilities do exist, they are usually unsanitary and poorly equipped and staffed.

One of India's biggest problems is child labour. At the moment there are one hundred million street and working children in India. The production of nuclear weapons cost the nation billions of dollars that could be put to better use in providing education and health for these children.

Joseph Jagan Devaraj, 24, India.

Many people living in poverty in India face a bleak future.

Photograph by Priyanka Khare, India

QUESTIONS & ACTIVITIES

1 Look at the table comparing data for UK and India. Choose four sets of data and produce pictograms for them. What do the differences indicate about the relative stage of development for these two countries? (5)

2 a Using the data in the table and the two case studies, what are the main differences between poverty in the UK and poverty in India? (5)

b Suggest some policies which could be pursued in the UK and India to help reduce poverty. (4)

3 Consumption

What Is Consumption?

Consumption is defined as the use of goods or services. It is a key component of economic thinking as it indicates the wealth of individuals or nations. One route to human development is to ensure that people consume enough so that they can live long, healthy and happy lives. The problem is that current consumption patterns are unequal and unsustainable.

UNEQUAL CONSUMPTION

During the 20th century, world consumption grew faster than anyone thought possible. In 1998 the world consumed $24 trillion of goods and services. Many people now enjoy a life of great luxury and are able to satisfy their every desire. However, more than one billion people have been left out of this consumption explosion and lack access to even the most basic goods and services, such as food, clothes, shelter and medical care.

For human development to occur, these people must be able to consume enough goods and services to meet their basic needs. Each benefit to an individual often also benefits the community: vaccinating one person against a disease reduces the chances of other people becoming infected; an educated individual benefits the whole community.

Consumption can have some negative effects on the consumer and others. If it involves toxic materials, it can cause pollution. It can also lead to exploitation of workers, greed, addiction, social rivalry, obesity and other health problems.

Over-consumption is the excessive use of goods and services. It is common in MEDCs and amongst the wealthier classes in LEDCs. As Gandhi said: "Our world has enough to satisfy everyone's needs but not everyone's greed." If people in LEDCs were to consume at the same level as people in MEDCs, we would need the natural resources of another eight planets.

RESPONSIBLE CONSUMPTION

Freedom of choice is seen as an important human right but it also brings with it certain responsibilities. The HDRs point out that there are often external factors which influence the choices we make, and the choices available to us. These factors include education, information, social barriers such as gender, ethnicity, culture, class, habits, language and household decision-making processes.

The richest 20% of the world's population consume 16 times as much as the poorest 20%.

Illustration by Julia Ortiz, 21, Peru

Consumption clearly contributes to human development when it enlarges the capabilities of people without affecting the well-being of others, when it is as fair to future generations as to the present ones, when it respects the carrying capacity of the planet and when it encourages the emergence of lively and creative communities.

(HDR 1998; p38)

Perhaps the greatest barrier to responsible consumption is that of habit. People do not like to change the way they do things, and will often go to great lengths to avoid change. Money is also a critical factor affecting consumption choices. The amount of money you have determines what you can buy. However, with money comes even greater pressure to make responsible consumption choices.

Aspirations

In the future
I want to have a very large house
With lots of rooms and bathrooms
No one will ever use
I wish to own lots of
The most expensive cars
Maybe one for each day of the week
And another for special events
I expect to have the most
Fashionable clothes
From the most expensive designers
And the most exotic jewellery
I hope I'm strong enough to wear it all
Oh! - I was forgetting the televisions and
the videos
I want at least thirty-five of each.
But behind each of my aspirations
I wonder if I am going to be rich enough
And I wonder if all these things are
necessary
To be happy, to be a good person,
Just to live?

Dominique Mansilla Hermann,
17, Argentina

Many people in LEDCs need to be given the opportunity to consume enough for a basic standard of living.
Photograph by Priyanka Khare, India

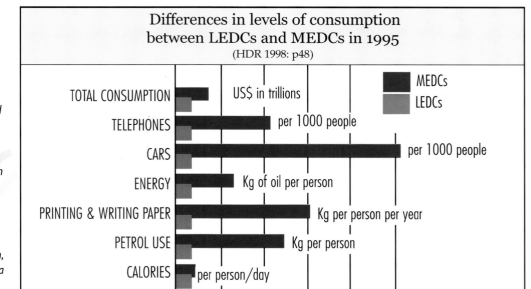

Differences in levels of consumption between LEDCs and MEDCs in 1995
(HDR 1998: p48)

MEDCs
LEDCs

TOTAL CONSUMPTION — US$ in trillions
TELEPHONES — per 1000 people
CARS — per 1000 people
ENERGY — Kg of oil per person
PRINTING & WRITING PAPER — Kg per person per year
PETROL USE — Kg per person
CALORIES — per person/day

Over-consumption leads to obesity and other health problems.
Artist unknown, Morocco

QUESTIONS & ACTIVITIES

1 What is consumption and why is it necessary for human development? (4)
2 What are the main problems with both over consumption and unequal consumption? (4)
3 List the main factors which affect people's consumption patterns. (5)
4 Look at the chart showing the differences in consumption between LEDCs and MEDCs.
a Rank all of the categories in order of greatest difference. (2)
b Discuss the ways in which these differences in consumption affect human development in LEDCs and MEDCs. (6)

Wants Versus Needs

When we consume, how do we decide what we really need rather than just what we want? This decision is influenced in many ways, by fashion, by how much money we have, and by advertising. Over-consumption is damaging to the environment and to society. In order for human development to take place it is important to learn to place less value on material possessions.

DEFINING WANTS AND NEEDS

There is a difference between wants and needs. Needs are things which keep us healthy and relatively happy, such as food, clothing, heat, housing, education and medication. Wants are things which are not essential but which we would like, such as holidays, televisions, cosmetics, sweets or fashionable clothes.

In many places around the world, people are surrounded by shops selling exciting things and bombarded by advertisements encouraging them to buy more things. These influences and other social pressures, such as fashion, can force people into accepting cars, televisions, mobile phones as the necessities of modern life. The widespread availability of cash points, credit cards and specialist shopping centres has made spending money easier than ever.

How we prioritise wants versus needs
(HDR 1998: p37)

BASIC EDUCATION FOR ALL *	6 BILLION
COSMETICS IN THE USA	9 BILLION
WATER & SANITATION FOR ALL *	8 BILLION
ICE CREAM IN EUROPE	11 BILLION
BEST HEALTH & NUTRITION FOR ALL *	13 BILLION
PET FOODS IN EUROPE & USA	16 BILLION

0   5   10   15   BILLIONS

* Additional annual cost of providing these basic needs for all

The luxuries of yesterday became the comforts of today and will become the necessities of tomorrow.
Illustration by Denise Smith, 13, Canada

ADVERTISING - THE ENGINE OF GREED?

Advertising is one of the most successful and profitable industries in the world today. Every year $1 trillion is spent worldwide trying to encourage people to buy goods which they often do not need or cannot really afford. The global advertising industry is growing a third faster than the whole of the world economy. Advertising can lead to feelings of greed, inadequacy, jealousy and competition - and it is all around us. Every time you turn on a television, listen to the radio or open a magazine or newspaper, you are bombarded by advertisements.

HOW CAN WE DEAL WITH IT?

The advertising industry does more than any other to promote unsustainable consumption patterns and the spread of information through advanced technology means that even small villages all around the world can be exposed to the consumption habits of the Hollywood elite. They are far more likely to have satellite television than a reliable road or railway link!

Although controlling or opposing the multi-billion dollar advertising industry is very difficult, efforts to curb advertising must be made if we are to have any hope of restraining people's spending habits, of healing the environment or of benefiting the poorest members of society. The key thing to remember is that the best things in life have always been, and will always be free.

The five countries which spent the most on advertising in 1996 (HDR 1998: p64)			
	ADVERTISING as % of GDP	EDUCATION as % of GDP	TOTAL ADVERTISING EXPENDITURE (US$ billions)
COLOMBIA	2.6	3.4	1.4
UNITED KINGDOM	1.4	5.5	16.6
NEW ZEALAND	1.4	6.4	1.0
HONG KONG, CHINA	1.4	2.8	2.2
KOREA, REP. OF	1.4	3.7	6.7

Religious Teachings On Consumerism

Putting limits on personal consumption has been encouraged in the texts and teachings of many religions throughout history.

° In Hinduism: "When you have the golden gift of contentment, you have everything."

° In Islam: "Riches are not from an abundance of worldly goods, but from a contented mind."

° In Taoism: "To take all one wants is never as good as to stop when one should."

° In Christianity: "Watch out! Be on your guard against all kinds of greed; a man's life does not consist in the abundance of his possessions."

° In Confucianism: "Excess and deficiency are equally at fault."

° In Buddhism: "By the thirst for riches, the foolish man destroys himself as if he were his own enemy."

HDR 1998: p40

I Want, I Want, I Want...

...a four-storey mansion with a kidney shaped pool, in a neighbourhood where you are no-one until you drive a Porsche. I want a country cottage five times as big as my home - which I'll never visit because I'll be stuck on the fifth floor of a down town office earning all my money. I want all my children in private schools, I want my wife in Paris and my mistress next-door. My life will revolve around other people's view of me and I'll want and want until there is nothing left that I don't possess.

Denise Smith, 13, Canada

I Need ...

...a room. A room with a bed and a chair and a table so I can eat and write. A pot and a small ring to cook on. I need food to eat, once a day, that's all, but food is so hard to find in the town and always we have so little money.

I need work to keep my mind busy - a job is too much to ask these days. I need clothes for my back and this is hard because many of the tailors have been killed or gone out of business. My one luxury is shoes as my feet are soft and get cut on our hard roads.

Sheku Syl Kamara, 21, Sierra Leone

QUESTIONS & ACTIVITIES

1 Think of one or two of your favourite adverts from the TV, magazines or the radio. What is it about them that you like? What makes you want to buy the product? Are your favourite adverts for things that you need or things that you want? (8)

2 Imagine you have to leave your home in a hurry after a fire or earthquake. In groups of 3 or 4, work out a list of the 10 things you would take. Each group can then report back, explaining their choice. Work out a top ten list for the whole class. (8)

How Long Can We Live Like This?

Without natural resources, human development cannot take place. Nearly a third of the world's population depend directly on renewable resources for their livelihood. However, current consumption patterns mean that renewable resources, such as soil, forests, fresh water and fish, are being used up by humanity far faster than nature can replace them.

SOIL

Since 1945, nearly one sixth of the world's productive land, over 2 billion hectares, has become degraded. This is due to it being over-grazed or over cultivated, and hedgerows or woodland being cleared so that soil just blows away. In the worst cases land becomes a desert and can no longer be cultivated to produce food or cash crops for sale. Almost 80% of the most degraded land is in LEDCs. If this degradation continues, there will soon be serious food shortages in parts of Asia and Africa. Each food shortage leads to more problems because the food which is available becomes more expensive and out of the reach of those who need it.

FISH

Since 1950, total fish catches have increased from 19 million tons to 93 million tons a year - a four-fold increase. New fishing techniques have almost destroyed some of the world's great traditional fishing grounds such as the North Sea, putting hundreds of local fishermen out of work. According to the UN Food and Agricultural Organisation (UNFAO), the fish stocks in 11 of the world's 15 major fishing grounds are proceeding rapidly toward total depletion.

Illustration by Problematika Rybolovu, Czech Republic

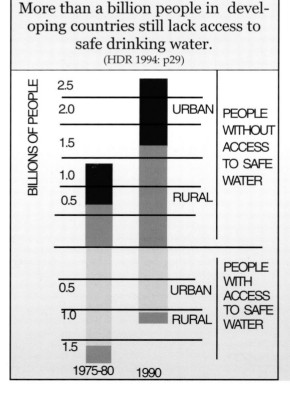

More than a billion people in developing countries still lack access to safe drinking water.
(HDR 1994: p29)

Graph — BILLIONS OF PEOPLE

	PEOPLE WITHOUT ACCESS TO SAFE WATER
2.5	
2.0	URBAN
1.5	
1.0	
0.5	RURAL

	PEOPLE WITH ACCESS TO SAFE WATER
0.5	URBAN
1.0	RURAL
1.5	

1975-80   1990

The Water Challenge

Water use has tripled since 1950, but its availability has declined dramatically from 16,800 cubic metres per person to 7,300 cubic metres per person. Underground reservoirs are running dry. At the moment twenty countries and 132 million people face severe water shortages, but if present trends go on, 25 more countries and up to 2.5 billion people will be affected by 2020.

The availability of clean water is both an environmental and a political issue. As water supplies become more limited, so the need to control access to them becomes greater and more difficult. In several parts of the world, nations are experiencing water 'overdrafts'. They are drawing more water out of underground aquifers or reservoirs than nature is able to replenish through rain and natural seepage.

Access to clean water also depends on political agreements between nation states and communities. For example, in the Middle East, every settlement has a quota of water it can draw from each well. However, serious disputes arise as the quality of water in each well varies. In parts of Israel, for example, some Arab communities complain that they are licensed only to use wells that contain salty, 'brackish' water which is impossible to drink and destructive to crops and soil quality if used for irrigation.

Destruction Of Forests

Case Study

Before the war (1992-1995) Sarajevo had many parks and boulevards with lots of trees. The hills and mountains that surround the town were filled with conifer forests hundreds of years old. However, during the war people were living without electricity and gas so they cut down the trees and used them for firewood. They used to go with saws and axes late at night, risking their lives to cut those trees because they had to find a way to survive.

Today the 'lungs of the city' are almost totally destroyed. The hills that surround Sarajevo are bare and without life. This problem is considered a local one for our town, but it concerns all Bosnia-Herzegovina. Investment in replanting forests is minimal and many forests are still being destroyed. In the 1950s forests covered 50% of the total area of the country but since then the forestry industry has processed 4 million tonnes of wood pulp per year.

The destruction of trees also affects the lives of people who live on the hills because it leads to erosion and landslides. In early February 1998, near Zenica, an industrial centre near Sarajevo, seven people died after their houses collapsed, as the direct result of erosion.

Unfortunately the problems caused by destroying forests will not disappear. They exist all over the planet. It is a problem of global dimensions. Why hasn't anything been done? People who could help just don't care enough. Cutting down trees is not just destroying beauty but destroying something necessary for us to live. We need to realise that and do something about it!

Selma Fazlić & Anisa Lojo, Sarajevo, Bosnia and Herzegovina

BOSNIA-HERZEGOVINA	Area: 51,129 sq km
Capital: Sarajevo	Population: 4,589,000

Illustration by Victor Sanjinez, 19, Peru

FORESTS

The clearing of forests, known as deforestation, leads to soil erosion, flooding, global warming and loss of the 'natural capital' of a country, yet trees are still being cut down at an alarming rate. An area three times the size of France, or 154 million hectares, of rainforest has been felled in the last decade.

Temperate forests are also being destroyed, which threatens to wipe out the last remaining areas of untouched forest in Europe and North America. Demand for timber is rising rapidly, but people are not replanting forests as fast as they are felling them. Worldwide, only one hectare is re-planted for every six felled, but the situation is worst in Africa where only one hectare is planted for every thirty-two felled. India is an admirable exception, replanting four hectares for every one felled. Both the environmental and human consequences of deforestation are huge, including shortages of fuel-wood and building materials, to microclimate changes, and loss of biodiversity and natural habitats.

QUESTIONS & ACTIVITIES

1 a Define renewable and non-renewable resources. Give examples of each. (4)
  b What human activities are causing renewable resources to be in short supply? (4)
2 a What are the specific problems with the loss of soil fertility and destruction of forests? (4)
  b What can be done to change things? (4)
4 a What is a 'water overdraft'? (2)
  b Why is the availability of clean water both an environmental and a political issue? (4)
  c What are some possible solutions to the problems of water quality and quantity? (4)

Consuming Differently

> *Is humankind heading for doomsday? Yes and no. The future is bleak if our consumption patterns continue at the current rate. But if we embrace existing alternatives, we can develop new patterns of consumption, new technologies and greater efficiency in resource use to make more resources available to poor people and minimise damage to the environment.* (HDR 1998, p81)

Fighting Consumption

All over North America, we are spreading like mushrooms. We call ourselves 'cultural creatives' and there are about 25 million of us altogether. We seek to consume less and live more lightly on the earth. I belong to a group called the North Olympic Living Lightly Society (NOLLS). We all aim to consume less but live more richly. This has to be the future for our planet and it is huge fun. We have found out about other sustainable consumption schemes around the world, such as co-operatives in Japan where groups of families unite to buy food from local farmers. Everywhere we look - in Europe, Latin America, Asia - there are more and more groups fighting consumption by living lightly on the earth.

Celeste Gilman, 15, USA

LIMITING CONSUMPTION

The 1998 HDR points out that, if current consumption patterns continue, in fifty years, global consumption expenditure will be five times as much as they were in 1995. The average consumer in MEDCs would spend over $55,000 a year compared to $20,000 today; pollution levels would continue to rise, with carbon dioxide levels more than doubling; and the crisis in renewable resources would become even greater. Educating consumers about how to consume sustainably is therefore very important. Achieving fairer patterns of consumption means reducing the over-consumption of most people in MEDCs whilst increasing the ability of those in LEDCs to consume enough to meet their basic needs.

SUSTAINABLE CONSUMPTION

Sustainable consumption has been defined as, "the use of goods and services that respond to basic needs and bring a better quality of life, while minimising the use of natural resources, toxic materials and emissions of waste and pollutants over the life cycle, so as not to jeopardise the needs of future generations." (Oslo Ministerial Roundtable: 1995).

Sustainable consumption can only be achieved through consumer education, like eco-labelling, but this is an uphill struggle against a $1 trillion advertisement industry. However, the success of The Body Shop, which has social and environmental criteria for all its products, shows that ethical products can still be commercially successful.

Eco-Labelling

Many labels don't explain where and how products were made; what they contain; their potential effects on our health; what their packaging is made from and how it can be recycled; or the impact they have on the environment and the people who produced them. 'Eco-labelling' is a way of giving consumers this information. Here are some examples:

The Soil Association mark is only for organic food produced without any chemical fertilisers, herbicides or pesticides.

No one knows yet the effect genetically modified food has on us or the environment so many prefer GM free food.

This symbol indicates that goods are either recyclable or contain recycled materials.

Many tuna tins are 'dolphin friendly', meaning that the tuna were caught in nets which did not also kill dolphins.

Products with the Freedom Food label come from animals reared, transported and slaughtered in a humane way.

The Forest Stewardship symbol is given to forest products which have been managed sustainably, not destructively.

The Fairtrade Mark is given to products where the people who grow the crop have been given a fair wage.

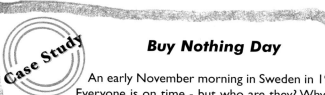

Buy Nothing Day

An early November morning in Sweden in 1997. Everyone is on time - but who are they? Why are they up so early? Yes, I know they look like creatures from the planet Mars, but in fact they are a gang of normal students. They have one aim for the day - to make people aware of what they are consuming.

The students decided to dress like Martians to walk around outside the biggest supermarket and find out what people have in their shopping bags. They asked customers what they had bought and why they had bought it. Some people got anxious and upset, but others were interested and sat down to discuss consumerism over a cup of coffee.

The day after, the students found themselves on the front page of two newspapers, and a week later the Environmental Deputy invited them to discuss local Agenda 21. Their action plan helped people realise that they buy a lot of things they do not need. On the next 'Buy Nothing Day', twice the number of people were involved in twelve countries. You are very welcome to join us next year. It's very fun and interesting!

Hanna Radberg, 23 , Sweden

Picture courtesy of Adbusters (www.adbusters.org)

CONSUMPTION IN LEDCS

Many LEDCs may not have had all the benefits of industrialisation and modernisation but this means that they can learn from the mistakes of MEDCs and see the effects of their dirty industries. They can start using new clean technologies to 'leapfrog' over the wasteful and polluting industrial processes of the past.

These new technologies include improved seeds which can raise crop yields; gas-powered cars and buses; low-cost water pumps and widespread immunisation programmes against preventable diseases. There is also a lot of research into innovations which can provide more output but which use less resources. Such technologies and innovations need to be supported by banks, governments and investment agencies in order to be successful and contribute to human development.

AdBusters

AdBusters is a Canadian group which challenges people's attitude to consumption through 'subvertising' - subversive advertising. They produce spoof versions of adverts by well-known fashion, food, tobacco and drinks companies, to make people think about the way in which the products were produced and question why they want to buy them. AdBusters has been trying to place advertisements on North American television showing consumers the social and environmental impact of their purchases and busting the buy, buy, buy messages of the other adverts. However, the television stations refuse to run the ads because they fear the big companies, whose commercials pay for their existence, will withdraw their ads in retaliation. Their experience proves that the opportunities for consumer education are limited by the market itself.

QUESTIONS & ACTIVITIES

1   Does your school have a policy to reduce, reuse or recycle? List some ways in which your school could reduce its environmental impact and consume more sustainably. (6)
2   Design a questionnaire to find out how much people know about sustainable consumption. You could include questions about whether they buy organic or fair trade food; whether they would be prepared to pay more for such products; whether they think they are influenced by advertising; whether it makes a difference to them where the things they buy come from; and what are the most important criteria for them in choosing the items that they buy. (10)

4 Population

Growing Trends

Population and levels of economic activity have increased more rapidly in the last four decades than at any time in human history. Since 1950, world population has grown from 2.5 billion to 6 billion. Most of that growth has taken place in LEDCs, where 77% of the world's people now live. (HDR 1992: p13)

CHANGES IN POPULATION

One of the most important global developments of the last century was the demographic transition, meaning changes in population structure. There were big changes worldwide in population sizes and population densities - the number of people living in a certain area. There has also been an increase in the population growth rate, although it is slowly stabilising now. Over the last fifty years, the natural increase - the difference between the birth rate (average number of births per 1,000 people per year) and the death rate (average number of deaths per 1,000 people per year) - went up dramatically.

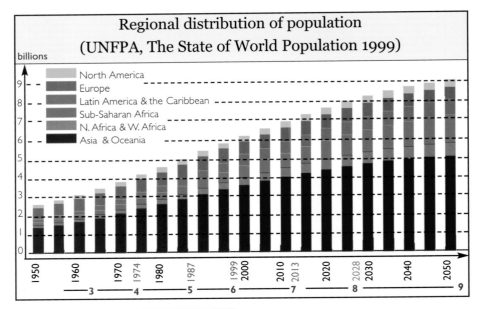

Regional distribution of population
(UNFPA, The State of World Population 1999)

billions

- North America
- Europe
- Latin America & the Caribbean
- Sub-Saharan Africa
- N. Africa & W. Africa
- Asia & Oceania

World population density
(UNFPA, The State of World Population 1999)

- Over 500 people per km²
- 200 - 500 people per km²
- 100- 199 people per km²
- 50-99 people per km²
- 10-49 people per km²
- under 10 people per km²

REGIONAL DIFFERENCES

There are huge regional variations in population growth rates. Most MEDCs are experiencing very low population growth rates. For example, between 1975 and 1997 the United Kingdom had an average annual population growth rate of 0.2% and it is projected to be less than 0.1% for the 1997-2015 period. In some countries population growth rates are zero or even negative, which means that the population is staying the same size or actually decreasing. Latvia registered an average annual population decline of 0.4% for 1993-2000.

NIGER
Capital: Niamey
Area: 1,267,000 sq km
Population: 10,961,000

Case Study

Africa's Population Bomb

Worldwide, the average number of children born per family is about 2.1. In Africa the average number of children per family is 5. In Niger, the number is 7 which means that the population is expected to triple from 7.7 million in 1990 to 21.5 million in 2025. Niger has difficulty feeding, clothing and finding jobs for its current population so these problems are going to be made even more difficult. It is the same situation in other African countries. This is Africa's population bomb.

At 4.4 people per square kilometre, Niger is one of the most underpopulated countries in Africa. Despite the recent increase in rural to urban migration as a result of droughts, 83% of the population is rural compared to 17% urban. In the rural areas there is always work to do, which is why families need to be large.

Ironically, for the majority of women in my country, abundant fertility is the greatest asset you can have because it gives you status. Infertility or sterility is the curse that every woman dreads. Sometimes, girls are encouraged to have children before they marry just to prove to prospective husbands that they are fertile. Even in towns our culture dictates that a woman's responsibility is to have the largest family possible. Any woman who resists this or thinks she would prefer to have a job and a career, is seen as odd.

The government of Niger is in some ways ahead of its people. They now recognise the value of educating young girls and are taking steps to do so. They also see the problems linked to teenage pregnancies and unwanted births, so they are introducing campaigns to prevent this and making serious efforts to slow down the rate of population growth.

Mireille Mignon, 15, Niger
(Translated from the original French)

The fastest population growth is taking place in LEDCs. Now they are suffering from over-population - too many people for the resources available. Africa has the fastest-growing populations of any region. The average fertility rate - the number of children born per woman - is more than five. At the beginning of the last century Africa's population was 118 million or 7.4% of the world population. By 1997 it was estimated at 778.5 million, more than 13% of the world's population. Africa's population is projected to be 1,453 million people by 2025, about 18% of the world's population . Asia is the world's most populous region with more than half the world's population, 3.6 billion people. Bangladesh has the highest population density in the world with 803 people per square kilometre.

PREDICTING POPULATION

Predicting population levels is very difficult, because it depends on so many factors. The United Nations uses three population projections, high, medium and low. Its medium projection for the world's population in 2050 is 8.9 billion. This calculation includes the impact of HIV/AIDS which, in countries like Botswana and Zimbabwe, has cut life expectancy by 20 years.

Another trend that could have a major impact is falling fertility rates in men. In Europe and North America, sperm counts have fallen by over 50% since the 1930s, due possibly to unknown toxins in the environment. If this trend continues, the problem for MEDCs won't be over-population but under-population - too few people for the resources available.

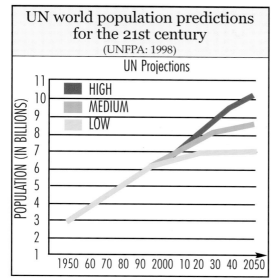

UN world population predictions for the 21st century
(UNFPA: 1998)

UN Projections

HIGH
MEDIUM
LOW

POPULATION (IN BILLIONS)

1950 60 70 80 90 2000 10 20 30 40 2050

QUESTIONS & ACTIVITIES

1 From the map on population density, can you identify ten countries with very high population densities? (5)

2 a What is natural increase and how is it measured? (2)

b Which region of the world has the biggest population growth rate? (1)

c Which two regions have very low population growth rates? (2)

3 a How accurate do you think population predictions are? (2)

b What policies could ensure that actual population growth is slowed to the UN's low projection? (4)

Population Challenges

Not all countries are experiencing the same changes in their population structure. However, both shrinking and growing populations present a challenge for governments and citizens. The HDRs point out that a stable and sustainable population is a key goal for human development.

No-one knows how many people the world can hold.
Photograph by Priyanka Khare, India

STAGES OF POPULATION GROWTH

A Demographic Transition Model (DTM) is used to analyse population growth by dividing it into four distinct stages. As countries become more developed they tend to move from stage one to stage four. Their population levels rise and then level off:

1. **Small population growth** - with high fluctuating birth and death rates;
2. **Rapid population growth** - when birth rates remain high and death rates fall;
3. **Slow population growth** - when birth rates fall rapidly;
4. **Stable population** - when birth and death rates are about equal.

THE GLOBAL SITUATION

Most LEDCs are at Stage 2 of the Demographic Transition Model while almost all MEDCs are now in Stage 4. Some MEDCs are even in a new Stage 5. Their death rates are higher than their birth rates so their population levels are actually declining.

What does this mean in practice? Countries with very high birth rates have large numbers of children under fifteen years old. As young people are often not earning any money they depend on their wage-earning parents to survive. The ratio of people who need to be supported by someone with a job, and the number of people who are working, is called the dependency ratio. Governments facing a high dependency ratio have to provide all their population, especially young people, with basic services such as schooling, medical care, including family planning, as well as jobs.

At the other end of the spectrum, countries with stable or declining populations, in Europe, Japan and North America, also have a dependency

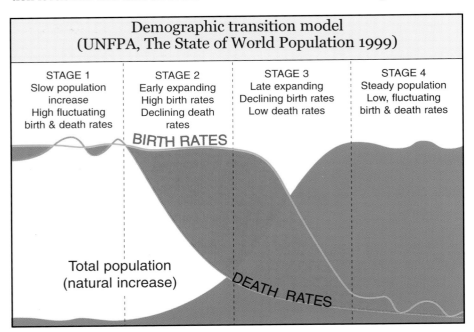

Demographic transition model
(UNFPA, The State of World Population 1999)

STAGE 1	STAGE 2	STAGE 3	STAGE 4
Slow population increase	Early expanding	Late expanding	Steady population
High fluctuating birth & death rates	High birth rates Declining death rates	Declining birth rates Low death rates	Low, fluctuating birth & death rates

BIRTH RATES

Total population (natural increase)

DEATH RATES

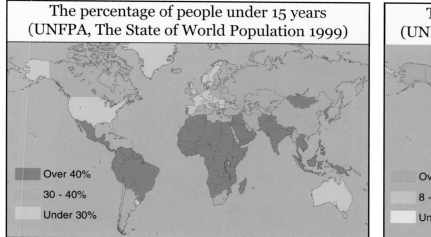

The percentage of people under 15 years
(UNFPA, The State of World Population 1999)

Over 40%

30 - 40%

Under 30%

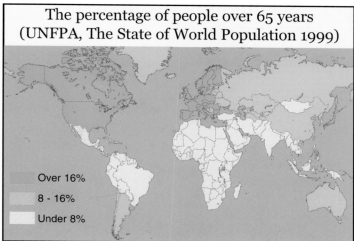

The percentage of people over 65 years
(UNFPA, The State of World Population 1999)

Over 16%

8 - 16%

Under 8%

problem. Although the number of people under fifteen years is low, the number of people over 65 is very high because people are living longer. Families are getting smaller and many people of childbearing age postpone parenthood to pursue their careers. The population is not renewed and the number of people over 65 years of age keeps increasing. Governments of these countries have to spend more money on providing support, medical care, residential homes and pensions for the elderly. Also they may need to encourage people from abroad to come into the country to do all the necessary jobs.

OTHER PROBLEMS

Demographic changes affect the economy, the environment, and the social and political aspects of a country. The HDRs point out that population growth is linked to many problems in LEDCs: poverty, limited services, unemployment and, particularly, the destruction of the environment. All these factors are inter-linked and the problem for LEDCs is that they continue to be in poverty while their populations continue to grow. This means that they have to do more with less: to improve living standards and provide social services, such as jobs, schools and healthcare facilities, for an ever-growing number of people, often on a smaller budget and a deteriorating natural environment.

Case Study

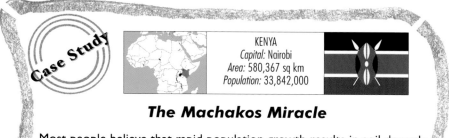

KENYA
Capital: Nairobi
Area: 580,367 sq km
Population: 33,842,000

The Machakos Miracle

Most people believe that rapid population growth results in soil degradation, forest clearance and ultimate desertification of a dryland region. The Machakos District in Kenya tells a very different story. Between 1932-1990 the population grew from 240,000 to 1,400,000. In 1930 soil degradation was a big worry. However, as the population grew, more people were available to construct terraces to conserve soil. By the 1980s over 8,500 km of terraces were being constructed each year - a process described as the Machakos Miracle. In addition, land values rose with the population, encouraging investment in high-yielding crops, integrating arable and livestock farming, and improving market infrastructure. This raised more money which enabled investment in schools and healthcare services, plus more indigenous and external advice on soil conservation. Between 1930 and 1987 arable land productivity rose six-fold; horticulture production rose fourteen-fold. Machakos demonstrates that a large population can be sustained through a combination of technological change, forward-thinking policies, and lots of local initiative and commitment.

(HDR 1998: p74)

QUESTIONS & ACTIVITIES

1 Describe the four stages of the demographic transition model and give an example of a country at each stage. (8)

2 a What is the dependency ratio (1)

  b Draw a table comparing the problems of too many old people with too many young people. (4)

  c Imagine you are a government minister of a country with a growing number of elderly people or young people who are economically non-productive. What difficulties might you be facing over the next 10-20 years and what policies could you use to deal with them? (6)

4 Use a copy of the last national census for your region. What kind of dependency ratio does it show? Conduct a debate within your class to discuss the results.

5 The Machakos Miracle in Kenya is not an isolated incident. Research two other areas where a high population density is also accompanied by high prosperity.(6)

What Are The Solutions?

Education, freely available, reproductive healthcare and child survival all promote lower fertility, thus creating the conditions for slower population growth and lower education and health costs in the longer run.(HDR 1996: p7)

REDUCING POPULATION GROWTH

In order to promote ways to reduce population growth it is necessary to look at the reasons why people have lots of children. People living in poverty often have large families because many of their children die prematurely and they want someone to support them in their old age. When women are overworked and have little time to do everything, they often want children to help them. Large families are therefore a way of coping with poverty. Reducing population growth means creating a situation where parents do not need so many children. This involves providing basic services such as clean water, sanitation and health care so that fewer children die, and expanding educational facilities and employment opportunities so that parents are encouraged to invest in the future of each child.

However, the most important factor associated with lowering the fertility rate is the education of women. A number of studies have proved the link between the education of women and the reduction of population levels and poverty.

Case Study

	CHINA
	Capital: Beijing
	Area: 9,572,678 sq km
	Population: 1,276,953,000

Population Control In China

China has a population of 1.2 billion according to the national census conducted in 2000. Population growth in rural areas has been higher than in urban areas so that now the rural population makes up 73.6% of the country's total.

In the 1970s family planning was introduced and the government encouraged each couple to have only one child. In urban areas couples, especially those who are well educated, usually follow the rules and have only one baby. This is also due to pressure from work. Some women working for foreign enterprises do not dare to become pregnant, especially when they have been promoted to a higher position, in case they lose their jobs.

In rural areas, where there is much poverty, couples have many babies. If you ask why they dare to violate the family planning policy they may say they need a son but their wife always gives birth to daughters. If the government wants to give them a fine they say they have no money.

One of the problems with China's family planning policy is that now the number of boys exceeds that of girls. Traditional Chinese culture says that the man is the master of the family so couples often want to give birth to a boy instead of a girl. In the past, when a pregnant woman found she had conceived a girl, sometimes her family persuaded her to have an abortion. To overcome this, in 1999 the Chinese government set out a rule that no hospital should tell a pregnant woman the sex of her conceived baby.

Zhao Yongli, 25, China

"You can avoid unwanted pregnancies."

Family Planning Agency, Niamey, Niger

VOUS POUVEZ EVITER DES GROSSESSES NON-DESIREES

PRENEZ CONTACT AVEC UNE FORMATION SANITAIRE

FAMILY PLANNING

Population growth can also be reduced by widespread voluntary use of family planning. Although there is much resistance to it - religious, cultural, financial, educational and logistical - without family planning, women have little or no control over the number of children they have or when they have them. Giving birth is often dangerous and there are high infant and child mortality rates in many LEDCs. Family planning facili-

Educating Girls Is The Answer

"Higher female literacy is associated with lower infant mortality, better family nutrition, reduced fertility and lower population growth rates."
(HDR 1990: p31).

Educating girls is the best way to reduce poverty and curb population growth. Countries which pursue gender equality enjoy faster economic growth while countries with a poor record of women in positions of power or influence have the worst figures for both economic and population growth. Putting girls in school reduces fertility rates, infant and maternal mortality rates, as well as raising economic productivity and improving environmental management.

Every year almost 12 million children under the age of five die of infectious diseases. Each extra year spent by their mothers in primary school lowers the birth rate, as well as the risk of premature child deaths and maternal deaths. In the southern Indian state of Kerala, where literacy rates are extremely high, the infant mortality rate is the lowest in the developing world. In Brazil, illiterate women have an average of 6.5 children, whereas those with secondary education have 2.5. However, 90 million primary school-age girls around the world are still not in school. Even if there were no other benefits, the education of girls should still be a cause worth fighting for because education is a human right.

Levels of female literacy and population growth
(HDR 1990: p31)

Bar chart showing POPULATION GROWTH RATE, % (left axis) and FEMALE LITERACY RATE, % (right axis) for MALI, AFGHANISTAN, YEMEN ARAB REP., THAILAND, SRI LANKA, JAMAICA.

To be born a girl in a rural area of countries such as Nepal, Pakistan, Algeria or Sudan often means a life without education, with early marriage and motherhood, children who die of preventable diseases, backbreaking work in the fields, and an early death. However, change is possible. In Guinea, Africa, pressure by the World Bank helped change school policy so that pregnant girls are no longer barred from returning to school and all new schools must have wells and latrines. As a result school enrolment for girls has gone up by 16%.

People living in rural areas often have large families to ease the burden of housework, such as collecting water from the well.

**Photograph by
Hadjara Kada Sani, Niger**

ties give women the opportunity both to limit the number of children they have and to decide when they want to have them.

The costs of providing contraceptives are very small compared to the costs of providing food, education and healthcare for thousands of children from unplanned births. It is cost-effective to pay for the expansion of family planning. At the UN's Conference on Population and Development in 1994, governments agreed to make family planning universally available by 2015. Over $17 billion dollars is needed for this but so far they have only provided $9 billion. More political will is needed to make it become reality.

QUESTIONS & ACTIVITIES

1 a Draw a star diagram to show why people may have large families. There are at least eight reasons. (8)
  b Which of these reasons do you think are the most legitimate? (2)
  c Read the article 'Educating girls is the answer'. What link does it make between female education and population growth? (4)
2 a Why are family planning services cost-effective? (3)
  b Look at the family planning case study abut China. Make a list of some of the obstacles to introducing family planning services in LEDCs. (5)
  c Design your own poster for a family planning campaign. Remember that there is a high rate of illiteracy in many LEDCs so words might not be appropriate. (5)

5 Settlements

A Changing World

More and more of us are deciding to live in cities. In the past 40 years the share of the global population living in urban areas has increased from 30% in 1960 to just over 50% in 2000. By 2015, it will be 61%. This process is called urbanisation.

URBANISATION

Urbanisation - the process whereby more people live in urban areas - has proceeded so rapidly that now there are not just cities but megacities. These have a population of more than ten million and most of them are in LEDCs. Urban areas in LEDCs are growing by one million inhabitants per week, whereas in most MEDCs urban populations are stabilising and, in some cases, even declining. All urban areas have their problems, such as pollution, unemployment and crime. These are made even worse in mega-cities, so why does the population of such places continue to grow?

There are two main reasons for the urban explosion witnessed in the twentieth century:

(1) Natural population growth - where birth rates are higher than death rates.

(2) Migration from rural to urban areas. This may be voluntary or forced.

In LEDCs migration into cities is due partly to rural 'push' factors - things which make people leave the country-side, and partly to urban 'pull' factors - things which make people want to move to the city. The problem is that when people do arrive in the city the reality is often very different from their expectations.

The biggest cities in 1800 and 1900, and megacities in 2000

(State of the World 1999 - A Worldwatch Institute Report on Progress Toward a Sustainable Society)

1800	(MILLIONS)	1900	(MILLIONS)	2000	(MILLIONS)
PEKING	1.10	LONDON	6.5	TOKYO	28.0
LONDON	0.86	NEW YORK	4.2	MEXICO CITY	18.1
CANTON	0.80	PARIS	3.3	BOMBAY	18.0
EDO (TOKYO)	0.69	BERLIN	2.7	SÃO PAULO	17.7
CONSTANTINOPLE	0.57	CHICAGO	1.7	NEW YORK	16.6
PARIS	0.55	VIENNA	1.7	SHANGHAI	14.2
NAPLES	0.43	TOKYO	1.5	LAGOS	13.5

Push and pull factors for urban migration

Rural Areas
PUSH FACTORS

- Eroded land - no way to make a living
- Not enough land available to distribute between big families
- Overcrowding
- No jobs: unemployment and under-employment
- Few educational facilities
- Lack of basic health services
- Exposure to natural disasters

Urban Areas
PULL FACTORS

- Better educational and health facilities
- More jobs available
- Higher wages
- Greater and more reliable availability of food and water
- More recreational facilities
- More comfortable housing
- A wider mix of people
- Access to government

Case Study

Rural To Urban Migration

After seven years without rain in north-east Brazil, Raimondo and his family were struggling to survive. A politician offers them free tickets to São Paulo if they will vote for him. There is no future for them in the countryside. Why not risk it?!

When he got off the bus, Raimondo realised the leap of faith they were taking. They had no money, no friends, nowhere to stay. They slept under a bridge for the first month, begging by day for food. It was humiliating. Raimondo went from house to house, looking for work. It was hard. Most of the time people did not even answer the door.

With the little money they earned he built himself a shack in a slum area of São Paulo. Their new neighbours warned them not to stay out late and to always obey the drug-dealers' rules. After a six-month struggle, they managed to get their children into a school. For a time, things seemed to be going well - then disaster struck. A terrible rain flooded the city. Raimondo was late home after his bus got stuck in a river of mud and garbage. A wave of mud had swept down the hillside, washing away all the shacks. They lost almost everything! They had to live in a shed with many other families. It was cramped, noisy and the smell was horrible.

Though there was much violence and drugs, they were lucky and avoided it. One day, a friend from the north-east was in town and told them of a new scheme to support farms near his old village. Raimondo thought about it. No, he realised, I am a city-dweller now!

Roberta Marquez Benazzi, 16, Brazil

BRAZIL
Capital: Brazilia
Area: 8,511,965 sq km
Population: 163,700,000

Street Dweller by Srijana Shrestha, 16, Nepal

REDUCING URBAN GROWTH

Controlling population growth and reducing migration to big cities are both important aspects of human development in LEDCs. As well as family planning services, governments should work to improve and maintain reasonable living conditions and increase opportunities in rural areas. They must increase rural people's choices so that they are not forced into the cities.

SUBURBANISATION

In many MEDCs it is the opposite problem. Instead of moving into towns people want to move away from the city to live in the countryside or in the areas on the outskirts of towns called suburbs. This has a big impact on transport, land use and the rural environment. For example, out-of-town shopping centres have sprung up all over Europe and North America. These are often built on agricultural or recreational areas of countryside. They require people to use their polluting cars to get there and contribute to the decline of city centres. Here the solution is to redevelop city centres to encourage people back into urban areas to live and work.

QUESTIONS & ACTIVITIES

1 a What is rural-to-urban migration? (1)
  b Why do many migrants to cities end up living in shanty towns? (4)
2   Write your own short story about someone in a LEDC who left their home in the country to move to the city. Explain why they decided to leave and what they expected to find in the city. (10)
3   Draw three bar graphs to show populations of megacities in 1800, 1900 and 2000 using different colours for countries in each continent. What do your results show? (6)

The Urban Challenge

In some ways, urbanisation is good for human development because large concentrations of people make it easier and cheaper to deliver goods and provide services. In other ways, it is bad for human development because towns and cities intensify the challenges of providing good sanitation and health services, employment and education.

THE COST OF CITIES

In 1992, the world's governments met in Rio de Janeiro for the Earth Summit. They discussed the world's problems and set out the solutions needed to deal with them. Each task had a price tag and the largest one was for settlements: $218 billion - over a third of the total budget.

Infrastructure for cities - sewerage systems, waste disposal, clean water and public transport - is very expensive. Often city authorities are unable to cope with the demands of the existing population, let alone the daily increase which happens due to migration. The mayor of Mexico City told an audience in Amsterdam, "My problem is that a new city the size of yours arrives on my doorstep every 3 months!"

In South Africa the problem is particularly acute. Under apartheid people were housed according to their skin colour. Row upon row of 'matchbox' houses provided adequate but soulless accommodation for blacks. Services such as water, sanitation and electricity were given to white people first. Today housing is a top priority for the government because there is a need for up to 2.5 million new homes.

SHANTY TOWNS

In many cities in some of the world's poorest countries, over half the population lives in shanty towns. Shanty towns are unplanned and unregulated semi-urban areas, often with no basic services. People who migrate into urban areas from the countryside and who cannot afford a house often build themselves a home out of what they can find and live in a shanty town.

Shanty towns are resilient and adaptable and are therefore not easy to remove. However, they are unpopular with urban authorities as they are often centres of crime, disease and pollution. Sometimes they try to clear away the houses but they are quickly rebuilt because people have nowhere else to go. Modern housing schemes now work with people already living in shanty towns. They encourage them to use their resources and skills to improve their own living and working environments, often using very eco-friendly, cheap building materials to build new homes.

Solutions to urban housing problems can be found in strong partnerships between local government, local businesses, and community groups. Promoting laws which support and protect shanty town dwellers, invest in them and ensure their participation in all decisions made, helps to secure solutions that will last.

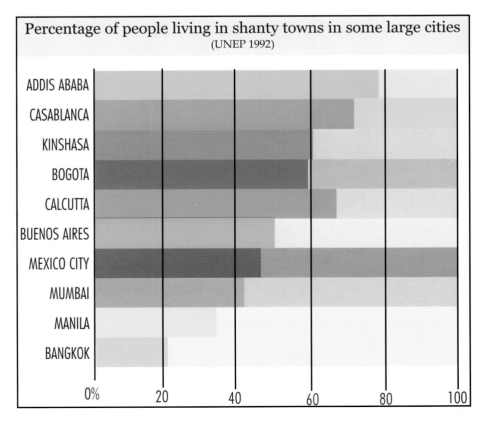

Percentage of people living in shanty towns in some large cities
(UNEP 1992)

ADDIS ABABA	
CASABLANCA	
KINSHASA	
BOGOTA	
CALCUTTA	
BUENOS AIRES	
MEXICO CITY	
MUMBAI	
MANILA	
BANGKOK	

0%   20   40   60   80   100

TANZANIA
Capital: Dar es Salaam
Area: 945,000 sq km
Population: 36,990,000

Dar es Salaam: Danger In Living

Residents in Dar es Salaam, the capital of Tanzania, have been warned that their habitat is not safe any more. Car fumes, industrial emissions, untreated liquid and solid wastes cause massive environmental pollution. A survey done by our Peace Child group along with experts and academic institutions reveals that Dar es Salaam is presently the least habitable urban centre in our country.

We identified air pollution as the biggest hazard. It is caused by lead-filled exhaust fumes emitted by old, badly maintained cars. There are also far too many cars for the congested roads of our city. The Tanzanian Licensing Board showed us records of an average of 60 new licenses for cars every day, not to mention commercial vehicles.

Waste

Dar es Salaam residents produce around 2,500 tons of solid waste each day, of which the city removes only 600 tons. There are no recognised dumping sites or landfills. This explains the huge garbage heaps that cover the city. Even city officials admitted at a seminar that, "The final safe disposal of hazardous industrial waste cannot be ascertained and continues to pose a threat to our citizens' health".

Unplanned growth

The city is growing out of control. Our survey discovered that 70% of residents live in squatter camps or 'unplanned areas'. These areas are characterised by unhealthy and squalid living conditions, dirty water supplies, lack of communication, little sanitation, lack of solid waste management and high crime rates. When people in such areas face very high unemployment rates, they can turn to crime to feed their families and themselves. Often that crime can be violent.

Housing demand far exceeds availability: 34% of citizens live in conditions designated as 'over-crowded'. Such housing, and the slum areas, are described by the authorities as 'low in supplies of oxygen'. Anyone who visits the Karikoo Market area on a busy day will know exactly what they mean.

Edward Mgalea, Tanzania

Waste disposal Is a major problem in urban areas, especially in LEDCs where councils cannot afford many public services.

Photograph by Drame Nima, Mali

THE FUTURE

The urban boom looks set to continue, although some measures may be able to slow it down. While urban areas can be centres of deprivation, they can also be centres of opportunity. Cities have half the world's population but generate two thirds of the world's income. The task is to make towns and cities work better as centres of human development. Key issues for urban management in the future include:

● Providing adequate housing for those with little money;

● Improving city services;

● Generating new employment opportunities;

● Healthier urban environments for all.

QUESTIONS & ACTIVITIES

1. Make a list of the problems faced by people living in cities in LEDCs. (4)
2. What are shanty towns and why are they so common in LEDCs? (4)
3. Imagine you are a member of the governing council in a city with a shanty town. Draw up a policy of how you would deal with it and the problems it causes. (10)
4. Considering the four key issues listed for urban management, draw up a strategic plan to address the problems faced by Dar es Salaam or your local town. (8)

Are Sustainable Cities Possible?

Imagine a city with no traffic congestion, without air or noise pollution, with clean water and healthy living conditions, with planned development and no poverty. A sustainable city full of happy, healthy and fulfilled people. Can such a city exist? Here we look at two attempts to create such a place.

BRAZIL
Capital: Brazilia
Area: 8,511,965 sq km
Population: 163,700,000

CURITIBA : PARADISE CITY?

Curitiba is the capital of Paraná, a southern state of Brazil. It is known as Paradise City and Brazil's Eco-Capital. Like all cities, Curitiba has had its challenges, but it has met them with innovative forward thinking and sustainable development policies.

Curitiba's population has trebled in 30 years so that it is now 2.5 million. It also suffered a decline in its traditional industries - coffee, tea and agricultural products. The city was facing disaster: economic collapse threatened to lead the city into the same kind of poverty and destitution that other cities in southern Brazil have suffered.

In 1972 the new mayor of Curitiba took a controversial step by stopping a motorway being built through the city centre and pedestrianising the main street. The citizens approved and he proceeded to 'zone' each section of the city as residential, industrial, commercial or mixed use. Limits, guidelines and controls were placed on each zone to ensure sustainable growth. Economic, environmental and social issues were given equal weight and

What are the benefits of sustainable urban planning policies?
(From 'The city of Curitiba, factors behind a success story'. Building and Social Housing Foundation, 2000. World Watch, Vol. 11. No 5, September/October 1998, How Mid-Sized Cities Can Avoid Strangulation)

AREAS	MEASURES	RESULTS
TRANSPORT	Preference for public transport and pedestrian streets. Designing the city's growth around a system of bus lines that minimise the need for cars.	75% of workers/commuters use public transport. Air pollution levels are amongst the lowest in Brazil compared to other cities of its size. Little traffic congestion, even though the city has the second highest per capita car ownership rate in Brazil.
ENVIRONMENT	Innovative waste recycling programmes. New sewage treatment programmes. Creation of parks, forests and open spaces. Environmental education activities. Citizen participation in environmental clean ups. Creation of permanent green space areas.	80% of solid waste goes to landfill; 20% is recycled. In London, 8% is recycled. The population co-operates in a recycling scheme called 'Cambio Verde'(Green Exchange). Cambio Verde exchanges recyclable trash for sacks of food, toys and teaching materials. Paper recycling is estimated to save 1,500 trees a day. Green area per inhabitant in Curitiba is 55 square metres compared to 4.6 square metres in São Paulo and 27.5 square metres in Belo Horizonte. Between 1993 and 1996 the number of people who were connected to a proper sewage system increased from 50% to 63% of the city's population, compared to 56% in São Paulo.
SOCIETY	Social care and support. Construction of the 'Lighthouses of Knowledge' (neighbourhood libraries). Programmes to educate and protect disadvantaged children. Housing provision.	In 1990 only 33% of Curitiba's population was in a low income band compared to 56.5% of Brazil's population. Forty Lighthouses (Libraries) have been built throughout the city, each providing 5,000 books. An average of 25,000 library cards have been issued at each Lighthouse. An estimated 7-20% of the population live in slums compared to 60% in Guyaquil, a town in Ecuador.
ECONOMY	In 1972, the Industrial City of Curitiba opened, stimulating a new economy based on manufacturing and service industries.	Before 1972 Curitiba accounted for 13% of Paraná's GDP. Today it accounts for 25% and is also responsible for 40% of the sales tax collected by the regional government.

importance in town planning decisions. Some of the policies adopted by the Curitiba authorities include:

- Promoting the use of public transport for going to the shops, to work, school, and to leisure activities;
- Improving the integration of the different sectors of the city by extending bus routes, gas, water and sewerage services;
- Limiting the town's pollution levels by controlling manufacturing and agricultural industries.
- Encouraging sustainable land use.

Many different groups from Curitiba, including the private sector, charities and citizen groups, were involved in the decision-making processes. This gave people a sense of involvement, responsibility and empowerment. The urban experiment in Curitiba continues, but up until now this city has proved very sustainable and successful.

The success of Curitiba has inspired many other cities to become sustainable cities. There are now several 'Eco-Cities' in the UK, such as Leeds and Peterborough. Town mayors and city officials now compete to win the highest eco-friendly credentials for their own settlements.

The city of Curitiba provides the world with a model of how to integrate transport, business development, infrastructure and local community development.

llustration by Narongchai Sithwatanaporn, Thailand

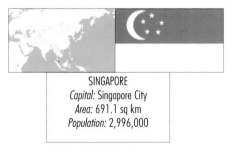

SINGAPORE
Capital: Singapore City
Area: 691.1 sq km
Population: 2,996,000

SINGAPORE: STRICT BUT SUCCESSFUL

Singapore is an island city-state in East Asia and is one of the world's most densely populated places - 4,360 people live on each square kilometre, compared to 241 in the UK. Official government policy aims to provide food, shelter, health and education for all its citizens. Singapore has been criticised for being a strict state with too many rules, regulations and limitations on what citizens can and cannot

do. Cars require a certificate of entitlement costing around $30,000 (£20,000) so many people don't own their own cars but use public transport instead. The state also has compulsory savings schemes for residents, strict regulation on building permits and tightly enforced laws against pollution. The result of all

this is that Singapore has one of the highest standards of living in the world. Home ownership is high, health and education facilities are excellent, and the city is clean and well managed. Perhaps even more remarkable is that this high standard of living is enjoyed by the majority of its residents and not just the privileged few.

QUESTIONS & ACTIVITIES

1 Why is it important to make urban areas more sustainable? (4)

2a What steps did Curitiba and Singapore take to effectively address the challenges presented by urbanisation? (4)

b What are the differences and similarities between the two cities? (5)

3 Look at the list of policy measures and results in Curitiba. Which do you think

were the two most important areas for introducing new policies and why? (4)

4 What examples of integrated planning can you see in the drawing by Narongchai Sithwatanaporn? (5)

5 Draw a map of either your town or an imaginary town and annotate it with the ways in which it could be made more sustainable. (10)

⑥ Globalisation

The Challenges

Never before have there been so many opportunities for links and exchange of resources between the peoples of the planet - airlines, phones, trade, tourism. This is globalisation, but is it a blessing or a curse? The speed of change is outpacing the creation of institutions to control it, threatening to reinforce inequality and marginalisation both within and between countries.

THE ORIGINS OF GLOBALISATION

Globalisation is not new. From the sixteenth century Britain, France, Spain and the Netherlands led the colonisation of other countries around the world by invading them, occupying them, and exploiting them to make themselves richer and more powerful. Many indigenous people and their cultures were persecuted in the process.

These colonial empires reached their height at the end of the nineteenth century then broke down during the twentieth century following two world wars and several national revolts. However, the injustice of colonialism set the stage for the continuing imbalances in the world today.

WHAT'S NEW TODAY?

The globalisation happening now is very different from the colonial era because, as HDR 1999 explains, it is shaped by new actors, new rules, new markets and new tools – each of which creates opportunities but also new challenges.

New Actors:

Transnational corporations are leading

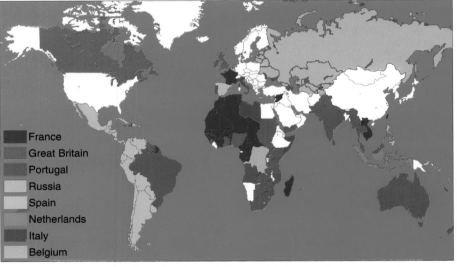

France
Great Britain
Portugal
Russia
Spain
Netherlands
Italy
Belgium

European empires dominated the world during the nineteenth century.

the integration of global trade, with $9.5 trillion sales in 1997 – that's 7% of global GDP. More regional and global organizations are becoming influential, from the World Trade Organisation to a growing number of regional trade blocs. NGOs are also networked and working together across the globe.

New Rules

More globally-based rules are being made. More and more international human rights conventions are being signed by governments. Agreements on the ozone layer, global warming and biodiversity have been negotiated. Market-based economic policies and democracy are being adopted in countries around the world.

New Markets

Financial markets now link worldwide traders and currency speculators in real time with instantaneous transactions. Consumers now buy global brands: Coca Cola and McDonalds are familiar to children from

Borders Are Disappearing - But For Whom?

Some people say that globalisation is making time, space and borders collapse into a global village. This is true for many people but not everyone. Financial dealers can send money instantly halfway across the world with little more than the touch of a button. For highly skilled workers international well-paying jobs are easily available. Many people from MEDCs can travel all over the world for holiday; and usually without complicated time-consuming visa procedures. Even NGOs can campaign around the world and use Internet networks to rally strong support for their causes.

However, unskilled/semiskilled workers who have to leave their homes to find work can end up with families divided across national borders. The majority of the world's people do not even have passports, and for those who do, obtaining visas to travel can be a long complex process. These people have yet to experience the many benefits of globalisation.

Vera Akatsa Bukachi, 19, Kenya

The Internet Divide
(HDR 1999: front cover)

South Asia | OECD (Organisation for Economic Cooperation and Development*)

Sub Saharan Africa

Arab States

Eastern Europe & the ex-Soviet States

Latin America & the Caribbean

East Asia | South East Asia & the Pacific

The large outer circle represents world population. The pie slices show regional shares of world population. The dark wedges at the centre show the number of Internet users.

* The Organisation for Economic Co-operation and Development is an Inter-governmental group of the world's 30 most prosperous trading nations. Headquartered in Paris, its members share a commitment to democratic governance and the market economy.

Manchester to Rio de Janeiro to Beijing. Technology has launched new service industries like telephones and internet-sales.

New Tools
Communication costs have plummeted because of the digital revolution: mobile phones and the internet are helping remote countries and communities overcome the constraints of their location and take part in global debates and business opportunities.

THE INTERNET - PROBLEM OR SOLUTION?

The growth of global telecommunications, particularly the use of e-mail and the Internet, is changing the way people live. Instant communication and an unlimited amount of information has transformed education, research, politics, and especially economics. The Internet decentralises power from traditional economic and political centres, helping combat global inequalities.

Small businesses can compete alongside bigger companies and ordinary people in different parts of the world can communicate and build up trade. For example, women in a village in Guyana, Latin America learned to sell their hammocks in the USA over the Internet and became the most successful business in the village.

The Internet allows the exchange of cultural knowledge, skills and ideas, and breaks down national stereotypes and barriers. However, most modern computer technology is still produced, and used, in MEDCs. This reinforces the marginalisation and poverty of LEDCs by creating a new 'information gap' to join all the other social and economic gaps. 80% of all websites are in English, yet less than one in ten people world-wide speaks it. To buy a computer costs a Bangladeshi more than eight years' salary; an average American will earn enough to buy one in just a month.

QUESTIONS & ACTIVITIES

1 a Ask 10 or 20 people who have Internet access where they receive emails from in a week. Plot this information onto a world map. (5)
   b How would this communication have been achieved 10 years ago or 50 years ago? How long would it have taken then and what were the implications for trade opportunities? (6)
2 Which countries are in the OECD? Why do you think that they have the highest rate of internet use? (4)
3 Create a spider diagram to illustrate the advantages and disadvantages of using the Internet as a tool for development. Include information about industry, commerce, business and employment (6)
4 Look at what's new about globalisation today. What opportunities and what challenges do you think they create for developing countries? (6)

The Solutions

Globalisation will have a fundamental impact on 21st century society so it is important to ensure it encourages positive rather than negative trends in human development. In order to guide the path of globalisation the HDRs identify seven key challenges.

WHAT IS GLOBAL GOVERNANCE?

Global governance does not mean a global government but a framework of rules, institutions and practices that encourage individuals, organisations, firms and governments to behave in certain ways. Until and unless the consequences of globalisation are managed at local, regional, national and global levels through better governance, the impact of globalisation on poor countries and poor people could be very harmful. The HDR 1999 suggests seven ways to promte-global governance.

1. DEVELOP NEW POLICIES

"Strengthen policies and actions for human development, and adapt them to the new realities of the global economy." (HDR 1999: p.9)

What kind of policies help encourage human development? Answer: economic growth that creates jobs, increases social and reduces military spending, promotes gender equality and respect for human rights and national cultures - and that doesn't destroy the environment .

2. STABILISE THE GLOBAL ECONOMY

"Reduce the threats of financial volatility - of the boom and bust economy - and all their human costs." (HDR 1999: p.9)

This involves trying to reduce the ups and downs of financial markets and minimising the devastating effects economic slumps can have on ordinary people's lives. Global financial markets must consider the social impact of their trading.

3. STRENGTHEN SECURITY

"Take stronger global action against global threats to human security." (HDR 1999, p.10)

Global threats such as international crime, environmental degradation, human rights violations and HIV/AIDS need to be tackled globally. However, this means that countries must actually stick to agreements made on international issues such as those on climate change made at the Kyoto conference in 1998.

4. TURNING TECHNOLOGY TO THE NEEDS OF THE POOR

"Enhance public action to develop technologies for human development and eradication of poverty." (HDR 1999: p.10)

Scientific research must shift from cosmetics for the rich to drought resistant crops and solar powered computers for the poor. The HDRs suggest launching an international campaign to boost research in LEDCs, and. to help them build their own technology capacity.

5. STRENGTHEN THE VOICES OF THE POOR

"Reverse the marginalisation of poor, small countries." (HDR 1999: p.11)

Poor and small countries need to actively participate in global discussions through associations such as the G77. This is a coalition of developing countries who have realised that they are more powerful when they work together to make their voices heard.

The different pillars of global governance.
Illustration by Idir Kerkouche, 24, Algeria

6. CREATE NEW STRUCTURES FOR INTERNATIONAL NEGOTIATIONS

"Remedy the imbalances in the structures of global governance with new efforts to create a more inclusive system." (HDR 1999: p.11)

Actions which could strengthen the position of many LEDCs against the power and influence of MEDCs include: independent legal advice; an impartial organisation to investigate injustices in global relations; policy research for LEDCs; regional institutions that work together politically and economically.

7. STRENGTHEN THE UNITED NATIONS

"Build a more coherent and more democratic architecture for global governance." (HDR 1999: p.12)

United Nations representatives should be elected and more accountable. Stronger links are also needed, between international institutions such as the World Bank and International Monetary Fund, which both fund development projects; the World Trade Organisation, which promotes international trade; and the United Nations Environment Programme, the world environment agency.

GOOD GLOBALISATION:

"Globalisation with ethics, equity, inclusion, human security, sustainability and development offers enormous potential for eradicating poverty in the 21st century." (HDR 1999: p1)

Globalisation can be used to promote human development. It can lead to higher incomes for people which results in them enjoying better diets, healthier lives and their children doing better in school. Although globalisation puts new pressure on them, governments should be encouraged to pursue pro-people growth. This recognises that human capital(people) are just as important as financial capital(money). If a country invests in a healthy, very well-educated, contented population, their citizens will be more likely to run successful businesses and participate constructively in civil society. Also, a prosperous community can afford to care for the natural environment.

Governments should support policies which create employment opportunities for people. Such policies include:
• removing taxes which prevent employers taking on more staff;
• setting up loan schemes to enable people to start up their own businesses; • promoting new industries, such as those dealing with computers;
• land re-distribution: when people farm their own land, they make it more productive and employ more workers.

QUESTIONS & ACTIVITIES

1 a Why is global governance not the same as a global government? (2)
b Why do the HDRs suggest that a system of global governance is necessary? (2)
2 Using all the information on these pages, make a list of the top five policies which you think should be pursued globally to promote human development. Give reasons why you have chosen those five policies. (6)

3 Use books or the Internet to research the G77. When was it set up, and what has it achieved? List at least twenty member countries. (6)
4 a What is pro-people growth and what policies could governments pursue to promote it? (4)
b Which of these do you think is the most important and why? (2)
5 What do you think are the main hurdles to achieving more and better global governance? (6)

Transnational Corporations

> *Transnational corporations (TNCs) control more than 70% of world trade and dominate the production, distribution and sale of many goods from developing countries. The UN Code of conduct for trans-nationals needs very careful monitoring.* (HDR 1994: p87)

THE PROBLEMS WITH TRANSNATIONAL CORPORATIONS

Transnational corporations (TNCs) are big companies with factories or offices in different countries around the world. They employ many people in LEDCs, but their headquarters, where important decisions are made and any profits go, are usually in MEDCs. Although they provide employment and goods and services that people need, such as food, water, transportation and shelter, TNCs face much criticism. Why is this?

The reason is that TNCs respond to their shareholders - people who invest money in the company to share in the profits. The main aim of shareholders is to make money from their investment, not to safeguard the environment or the company's workers overseas. This puts pressure on the practices and ethics of TNCs. For example, tobacco

My Country Is Not My Own

Throughout my life I have been aware that my country is a playground for rich people to exploit. The businessmen and tourists crowd my streets, lie on my beaches, fill my hotels, museums and restaurants. They benefit from our hard labour. It is they who drive cars while I walk. It is they to whom we beg to hire our services as guides and beach boys. How do I feel about it? Not happy. It is as though my country is not my own.

Ellery Katisi, 17, Tanzania

TNCs hid the truth about the health risks of smoking for many years, and mining or timber companies often contribute to the destruction of the environment. Some TNCs form groups to protect their economic interests, ignoring wider social or environmental issues. Oil companies and car manufacturers both fought against climate change negotiations to reduce carbon emissions in case it forced people to use their cars less.

TNCs AND EMPLOYMENT

"Transnational corporations employ over 22 million people outside their headquarter countries, of whom almost 7 million are employed in developing countries. That is less than 1% of the economically active population - not a great contribution to poverty eradication."
(HDR 1992: p35).

TNCs usually employ only the most highly educated and skilled people in LEDCs. When they do employ unskilled workers, there are often no regulations on pay or conditions so people can end up working long hours in difficult or dangerous conditions for very little money.

TNCs ARE CHANGING

However, TNCs are becoming more responsible and introducing voluntary self-regulation. An agreement has been made between TNCs and the United Nations to work together more closely. For example, when developing the Montreal Protocol, an international convention to reduce ozone depletion, the UN worked closely with TNCs to help industries in LEDCs replace CFC-based refrigerators and air conditioners. The Montreal Protocol's targets have now been exceeded.

In 1997 the top TNCs had sales totalling more than the GDP of many countries. (HDR 1999: p32)			
COUNTRY OR CORPORATIONS	GDP OR TOTAL SALES (US$ BILLIONS)	COUNTRY OR CORPORATIONS	GDP OR TOTAL SALES (US$ BILLIONS)
GENERAL MOTORS	164	ROYAL DUTCH/SHELL	128
THAILAND	154	MARUBENI	124
NORWAY	153	GREECE	123
FORD MOTOR	147	SUMITOMO	119
MITSUI & CO.	145	EXXON	117
SAUDI ARABIA	140	TOYOTA MOTOR	109
MITSUBISHI	140	WAL MART STORES	105
POLAND	136	MALAYSIA	98
ITOCHU	136	ISRAEL	98
SOUTH AFRICA	129	COLOMBIA	96

Tourism

Tourism is the world's biggest industry. It can be one of the most beneficial industries for LEDCs, bringing in much needed investment, but it can also be one of the most damaging. If the business is dominated by transnational corporations, such as tour operators and hotel chains, many of the profits and benefits may not reach local businesses or people.

THE PROBLEMS WITH TOURISM

The problem with tourism is that it often leads to the destruction of the very places people want to visit. Air travel has made travelling around the world cheap and easy for those who can afford it, but it is one of the biggest sources of atmospheric pollution. As tourist destinations become more popular they become more built up as TNCs come in to build airports, roads, or hotels. This often takes away valuable resources, such as clean water, from the native population. Also, tourists are not always interested in the local culture of where they are staying treating it as a source of entertainment.

THE BENEFITS OF TOURISM

LEDCs have considerable natural endowments, such as sunshine, rich cultures or national parks, all of which can encourage tourism. Most governments promote tourism and remove barriers to international and internal travel. For many LEDCs tourism is an important source of foreign currency and employment. In 1996 the world-wide tourism industry provided 250 million jobs and had sales of $3.6 trillion. By 2006, it is forecasted to provide 385 million jobs and sales of $7.1 trillion. Currently it employs 10% of the world's workforce. It is also a popular sector for investment. For example, in Eastern Europe investment in tourist infrastructure is expected to grow by 140% between 1997-2007.

The tourism industry is facing up to its environmental challenges by promoting initiatives like 'Green Globe' and 'Eco-tourism'. These initiatives call on countries to assign economic value to natural and cultural resources, such as animals, forests, buildings and traditional

Tourism in Cyprus, by Michael Troukides, 17, Cyprus

ways of life, that are normally seen as having none. Finally, tourism could also help promote peace and international understanding. With the right environmental and cultural controls it could become a powerful force for good in the future.

QUESTIONS & ACTIVITIES

1 a Look at your clothes' labels. Where were they made? (4)

b Find out where the company's headquarters are, compared to where their factories are. Put this information onto a world map. (6)

c Why do TNCs prefer to locate their factories in LEDCs and their main offices in MEDCs? (5)

2 Complete a cost-benefit analysis for tourism in your area or a famous tourist destination such as Disney Land or the Costa Del Sol. (8)

3 a What do the terms *sustainable tourism* and *eco-tourism* mean? (4)

b Research some examples of where tourism has helped a community and local environment. (6)

Sustainable Development

> *Any form of debt - financial debt, the debt of human neglect, the debt of environmental degradation - is like borrowing from future generations. Sustainable development should aim at limiting these debts.* (HDR 1990: p7)

WHAT IS SUSTAINABLE DEVELOPMENT?

Sustainable development has been famously defined as, "Meeting the needs of today's generation without compromising the ability of future generations to meet their needs" (Our Common Future, 1992). The former UK Environment Minister, John Gummer, simplified this to, "Not cheating on your children". There are currently six billion people living on earth. Sustainable development is concerned with how we should manage the resources of our planet to feed and provide livelihoods for those six billion, and the billions yet to be born.

Sustainable development is a process in which trade, energy, investment, agricultural, industrial and environmental policies all need to be linked. The 1992 HDR identifies the basic principles of sustainable development as the reduction of population levels, elimination of poverty, redistribution of resources, healthy and well educated people, decentralised, participatory government, fair trading systems, and better environmental understanding.

THE ENVIRONMENT

Sustainable development is often associated with protecting natural resources and the physical environment. However, the HDRs have always shown environmental issues are linked to human development. Environmental degradation has the greatest impact on the poorest people while at the same time poverty is one of the greatest threats to the environment, causing deforestation, desertification and pollution. The main priori-ty of most people living in poverty is to provide food and shelter for their families, not saving the environment. Any environmental policies must therefore include plans to reduce poverty.

Essential policies which should be encouraged are the transfer of eco-friendly technologies from MEDCs to LEDCs and the control of pollution levels through banning certain types of pollution and making polluters pay for the environmental damage they cause.

AGENDA 21

In 1992 there was an Earth Summit, a meeting of world leaders to discuss the future of the planet, in Rio de Janeiro, Brazil. There it was agreed to make sustainable development the central organising principle of the United Nations and to re-orientate education towards it. The world leaders came up with a 40-chapter document for achieving sustainable development called Agenda 21. The total cost of making the world more sustainable was calculated at around $600 billion. This seems like a lot of money, but Agenda 21 argued that when the survival of the planet is at stake, such spending should be an absolute priority.

However, by 1997 the Global Environmental Facility, set up to manage funds for environmental improvement, had received only $2 billion for Agenda 21 spending. Also, despite the promised increase in overseas development aid to poorer countries, the amount given actually decreased between 1992-1997. Governments aren't doing their part so it's up to their citizens to encourage their leaders to live up to their promises and commitments.

Involving Young People In Agenda 21

"The involvement of today's youth in environment and development decision making and in the implementation is critical to the long term success of Agenda 21!" (Chapter 25, Agenda 21)
Young people have to be involved in Agenda 21. It is a must and governments have to make it happen. In Plymouth the City Council embraced this challenge by setting up Plymouth Young People's Agenda 21 or PYPA 21. PYPA 21 represents young people's views on environmental issues and works in partnership with other groups in the area.

I was involved in PYPA 21 for three years and really enjoyed it. From beach clean-ups on summer days, to book editing, to promoting fair-trade goods, to organising one day conferences, to running workshops on everything from water pollution to development issues - I got involved and helped make a huge difference to the local community. PYPA 21 was always interesting, exciting and varied, but, most importantly, it was always fun. After the Rio Earth Summit, several councils set up Local Youth Agenda 21s. Sadly, many of these have disappeared - victims of budget cuts. PYPA 21 continues- a great example of how a local authority can mobilise young people to improve their communities in a sustainable way.

Tom Burke, 16, Plymouth, UK

HOW DOES IT WORK?

So what does sustainable development look like in reality?

Conservation: Conservation of the environment, including biodiversity, water, fisheries, soil and energy, is at the heart of sustainability. A sustainable society is one that sees waste as a resource which does not yet have a use. The motto is: reduce, re-use, repair, recycle.

Factor Four: The idea of Factor Four is to get twice as much energy or productivity out of half the amount of resources. A good example of this is the longlife light bulb. It gives the same amount of light as an ordinary light bulb for a tenth of the wattage and lasts 10-20 times as long. Another example is a car that can go 200 miles on a litre of petrol. Now people are looking for technologies that can deliver factor ten, even factor fifty, savings. This is where money can be made in the future and it is at the heart of the search for a more sustainable society.

Measuring Sustainability:
The success of sustainable development policies depends on the way their effects are measured. The UN and some governments have been exploring different 'Sustainability Indicators' and ways of 'Green Accounting'. This is a way of treating the environment like capital, or money in a bank. If you cut down a rainforest or run a well dry you are using up capital. If you use renewable energy, and re-plant the forests you cut down, you are conserving capital and that is a more sustainable way of running a society.

Some governments in LEDCs are more concerned with rapid development than sustainability. They seek quick growth in their economy's productivity. This often involves drawing on environmental resources such as forests, coals, oil reserves, fish and minerals. If these resources are exploited to excess, the damage can set development back. The challenge is to find the balance.

The catch-phrase of sustainable development is "Think Globally: Act Locally."

Illustration by Stephen Sehlage Swalopund, 17, Namibia

QUESTIONS & ACTIVITIES

1 a Make up your own definition of what you understand by sustainable development. (3)

b Make a list of six reasons why it is so important. (6)

2 a How are environmental issues linked to human development? (4)

b What policies can be pursued to help protect the environment? (4)

3 Research what was agreed at the Rio Earth Summit (also called World Summit on Sustainable Development). Can you find out how much has been achieved? (8)

4 Look at the picture above and find as many examples of sustainable and unsustainable lifestyles as you can. (6)

7 The Global Economy

The Politics Of Aid

One of the ways in which governments of MEDCs seek to balance the huge inequalities between themselves and LEDCs is to transfer money and goods through Overseas Development Assistance (ODA), also called aid.

TYPES OF AID

There are many different types of aid. *Short-term aid* is given in emergencies to deal with immediate problems, such as food during a famine. *Long-term aid* is used for more specific projects, like hospitals or schools. *Multilateral aid* is when several countries give money to a central agency, like the United Nations Development Programme, which then distributes it. *Bilateral aid* is where one country makes a donation directly to another. There is also *tied aid* where money has to be spent on goods from the donor and *untied aid* which the recipient country can spend as it wishes.

THE PROBLEMS WITH AID

"ODA has critical weaknesses in quantity, equity, predictability and distribution." (HDR 1992: p44)
There are no binding agreements about where aid should be given and what it should be used for. If LEDCs become dependent on aid they are at great risk. Their economies could collapse if the aid supply is cut off. Aid must be used by LEDCs to develop their own sources of income.

Quantity: The UN set a target for all MEDCs to give 0.7% of their GNP as ODA each year. The average among donors is a third of this, 0.25% of GNP, US$55 billion a year, roughly what Europeans spend on cat food.

Equity: Only 27% of ODA goes to the countries which are home to 1.5 billion of the world's poor. About 60% of ODA goes to just five countries: India, China, Bangladesh, Egypt and Israel. The HDRs call for a target of at least 0.15% of MEDCs' GNP to go to the world's least developed countries.

Predictability: Donors can cut off aid at a moment's notice. They can use aid to promote their own technologies or skilled professionals, or to strengthen strategic alliances. Aid is sometimes given to countries with large military budgets encouraging them to buy arms, not help their poorest people.

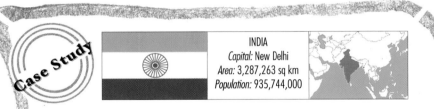

Case Study

INDIA
Capital: New Delhi
Area: 3,287,263 sq km
Population: 935,744,000

The Narmada Dam In India

The Narmada Valley Project in Western India is one of the world's most hotly contested development projects. It is being funded by the Gujarat state government using ODA. Advocates of the plan say that the thousand dams on the Narmada river will provide water to drought-prone areas and convert millions of hectares of barren land into fertile and cultivable farmland. The protesters point out that the dams will submerge large areas of land that is already cultivated.

Local tribal people, who have been living sustainably in the old ways of the forest for centuries, will have their land taken away from them and most people will not be eligible for relocation. Also the rich flora and fauna of this biodiversity hot spot will be lost. Every submerged acre may mean the loss of a cure for cancer or AIDS.

To my mind, this is inhuman, unsustainable development: the tribes of Bhils, Bheladas, Gonds, Korjus, Kirs and Bhaiyas will be thrown off their ancestral lands, and left without their traditional livelihoods. Their lot will be 'improved' by wrenching them away from their centuries' old sustainable lifestyles into the modern, fashion-conscious consumerist world of which they have no experience.

Juhi Nagarkatti, 16, India

Distribution: Sometimes aid is given to visible projects such as big hospitals, universities, roads or dams rather than to rural schools, water supply or health clinics where funds would benefit more poor people.

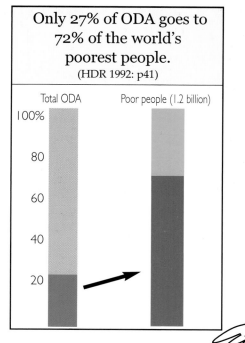

Only 27% of ODA goes to 72% of the world's poorest people.
(HDR 1992: p41)

Total ODA | Poor people (1.2 billion)

100%
80
60
40
20

FOREIGN DIRECT INVESTMENT (FDI)

While the amount of ODA given to LEDCs fell during the 1990s the amount of Foreign Direct Investment (FDI) - money invested in countries by outside companies - tripled. However, FDI is concentrated in a few of the richer countries. In 1998 it was worth $280 billion but only 3.6% went to Sub-Saharan Africa and less than 1% went to the world's forty nine poorest countries. Investors put their money where there is an educated work-force, a stable or growing economy, and where they are most likely to get big profits.

NON-GOVERNMENTAL ORGANISATIONS (NGOs)

"NGO activities today touch the lives of about 250 million people in developing countries" (HDR 1993, page 93)

Non-Governmental Organisations (NGOs), like OXFAM, the Red Cross /Red Crescent or Save the Children, work independently from governments and official development agen-

A ceramic business in Peru funded through a microcredit scheme.
Photograph by Tom Jolly, UK

Microcredit: Helping People Help Themselves

Both governments and aid agencies are now realising that microcredit schemes are a powerful way to eradicate poverty. They lend small amounts of money to people who cannot get loans from commercial banks to start or expand their own small businesses. Loans may be spent on a cow, a sewing machine or renting a stall at the market.

Such schemes have been phenomenally successful. For example, the Grameen Bank in Bangladesh lends money primarily to landless rural women and has a repayment rate of 95% - much higher than what the mainstream banks achieve. This is because the women support each other as a team, ensuring that everyone makes their repayments.

'Trickle Up' is a US-based international microcredit charity which not only lends money to people but trains them in how to start-up and run a business successfully. Since its founding in 1979, Trickle Up has helped to initiate more than 38,000 small businesses in 18 LEDCs.

cies. The advantages of NGOs are that they are often less politically-motivated and more cost-effective than government-funded programmes. Also, they can respond quickly to emergencies and introduce education, healthcare and income generation schemes to more remote rural communities or marginalised groups.

QUESTIONS & ACTIVITIES

1 a What are the different forms of aid? (3)

b Why is dependency on aid a problem? (2)

c What are the four problems with aid identified by the HDRs? (4)

d Do you think aid is most effective as short term help or long term support? Give the reasons for your answer. (6)

2 Why do microcredit schemes work so well? (4)

3 Design a questionnaire to find out people's opinions on aid. How many people make donations, and to which charities or causes? What would encourage them to give more? Present some of the results in the form of a graph of your choice. (8)

The Trading Game

Global markets are not friendly to poor nations. Developing countries enter the market as unequal partners and leave with unequal rewards. (HDR 1992: p68)

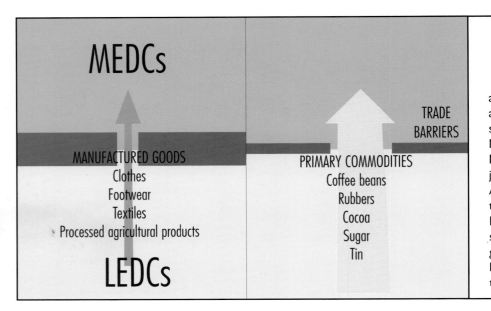

MEDCs

MANUFACTURED GOODS
Clothes
Footwear
Textiles
Processed agricultural products

LEDCs

PRIMARY COMMODITIES
Coffee beans
Rubbers
Cocoa
Sugar
Tin

TRADE BARRIERS

Unjust Trade Barriers

Trade barriers have long worked against LEDCs, especially in textiles and agriculture. Cheap labour makes some LEDCs more competitive than MEDCs in these industries but the MEDCs use tariffs because they fear job losses at home. The Multi-Fibre Agreement, for example, has long protected textile manufacturers in the MEDCs against LEDC competition and so has stopped LEDC industry from growing. Although the MFA is now being phased out, it has set back LEDC textile opportunities by many years.

THE HISTORY OF TRADE

Trade began when the first groups of human beings started to exchange goods. It then increased in importance over the next few thousand years. From the fifteenth century onwards trade was tied up with colonialism as the European countries invaded and occupied much of Africa, Asia and South America. The slave trade shipped 12 million slaves from Africa to the Americas to work on plantations, with 2 million of them dying on the way. The ships returned to Europe with products like tobacco, sugar or coffee. Europe grew rich from its colonies and slave labour.

TRADING TODAY

Today the international trading system is more complex but it is still most beneficial to the richer and more powerful countries. The 1992 HDR estimates that the current trading system is so unfair that it actually costs LEDCs over $500 million a year. This is ten times what they receive in ODA. Therefore a fairer system of international trade would benefit poor people more than just increasing ODA.

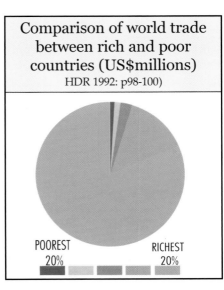

Comparison of world trade between rich and poor countries (US$millions)
HDR 1992: p98-100)

POOREST
20%

RICHEST
20%

Many LEDCs are dependent on the export of a few primary commodities. The prices for these are unstable so they often have to sell them for little money. LEDCs also face many trade barriers when exporting processed agricultural products and textiles to MEDCs. These are designed to discourage them from processing their raw materials. MEDCs can buy raw materials from LEDCs, process them into manufactured products and then sell them back to LEDCs!

THE SERVICE SECTOR

MEDCs also dominate trade in the fastest growing sector of the global economy, the service sector - travel, communications, financial services, advertising, tourism and media. Although these are labour-intensive industries, they still demand and depend on technology so few LEDCs have a chance to compete. Some

Brain Drain

In years gone by Sri Lankans used to send their children to European and American universities to get degrees. As graduates, they would return to Sri Lanka to lead a comfortable life using their much sought-after knowledge.

Today, Sri Lankan parents still strive hard to do the same thing, but only so that their children may find a job in a developed country and raise their future families in a safe, modern environment sending much-needed money to their families at home.

Part of the reason is the rising number of unemployed graduates. There are so many strikes and student rebellions because they wait up to two years to get into university only to find when they have their degree, there are no jobs for them. Brain Drain is a phenomenon which is continuously sapping the Sri Lankan genius.

Ermiza Tegal, Sri Lanka

LEDCs can compete, like India in the computer software market, where there are motivated entrepreneurs and highly skilled programmers, often returning from abroad.

CHANGE THE RULES

"Fundamental reforms are needed for global markets to benefit all nations and all people." (HDR 1992: p68)
Part of the solution to the unfair system of trade is for LEDCs to diversify their economies and reduce their dependence on a few exports. Unfortunately this is a vicious circle because LEDCs need money from their exports to invest in new industries and train people to work in them.

BRAIN DRAIN

Each year LEDCs lose thousands of engineers, doctors and scientists to MEDCs where they can earn more money and enjoy a better standard of living. They are frustrated by low pay in their own countries. This only makes it more difficult for LEDCs to climb their way out of poverty though education.

A Peruvian farmer inspecting coffee beans before they are roasted. He is a member of a co-operative of coffee farmers.

Photograph courtesy of Café Direct

Who earns what from each jar of coffee sold?

£1 (100p):

FARMER: 10p

TRADER: 20p

SHIPPING MERCHANT: 10p

IMPORTER: 20p

GOVERNMENT: 20p

RETAILER: 20p

Ugandan Coffee

I am a native of the slopes of Mount Elgon where coffee is the main cash crop. Peasants in this region struggle so much to grow coffee. They prune, weed, spray and harvest. It is extremely hard work but when the harvest is done the price of the coffee is never announced to the farmer. There is always talk of problems with the exchange rate of the dollar, and farmers are always told to accept a lower price. In this way, the morale of farmers is very low. These days, globalisation is a big threat to us.

David Lyada, Uganda

Fair Trade

Guarantees
a **better deal**
for Third World
Producers   Fairtrade

Much of the food and drink we have every day, such as coffee, tea, chocolate and fruit comes from LEDCs. The current system of international trade means that the people who grow the crops for these goods get very little of the profits. For every pound spent on a jar of coffee in a MEDC, the farmer who actually grew and harvested the beans only gets 10p. The rest goes to the people who transport, process and sell the product.

A solution to this problem is fair trade where the company buying the crops pays a decent minimum wage to the workers growing them and works with them to improve living and working conditions. In Britain an organisation called the Fairtrade Foundation has set up a Fairtrade Mark so consumers can tell which products have been fairly traded. Look for it in your shops now!

QUESTIONS & ACTIVITIES

1 a Why were European countries so keen to acquire colonies? (4)
  b How did colonisation help shape the current trading system? (4)
2 a Why is it so difficult for LEDCs to improve their trading prospects? (2)
  b Why does the UK charge only a small tariff for coffee beans to be imported and a large tariff for manufactured coffee in a jar or tin? (2)
3 a Look around your house at where some of the products you have, such as food, electrical equipment and ornaments, have come from. Draw up a table to show your results. What patterns do you see? (4)
  b Turn your results into a map showing imports into the UK. (8)

A Fate Worse Than Debt?

The debt crisis is one of the biggest obstacles to development for the poorest countries in the world and is another part of the unfair world trading system. It is the modern equivalent of the slave trade because it benefits the richest countries of the world at the expense of the poorest.

THE DEBT CRISIS

The debt crisis started when banks in MEDCs lent money to LEDCs but most debts are now owed to international financial institutions such as The World Bank and the International Monetary Fund (IMF). These were set up after the Second World War to support countries having financial difficulties. However, the loans were conditional on the imposition of Structural Adjustment Programmes (SAPs) which forced countries to reduce their spending on schools and health-care and expand cash crops for export. SAPs have actually made poverty and inequality worse.

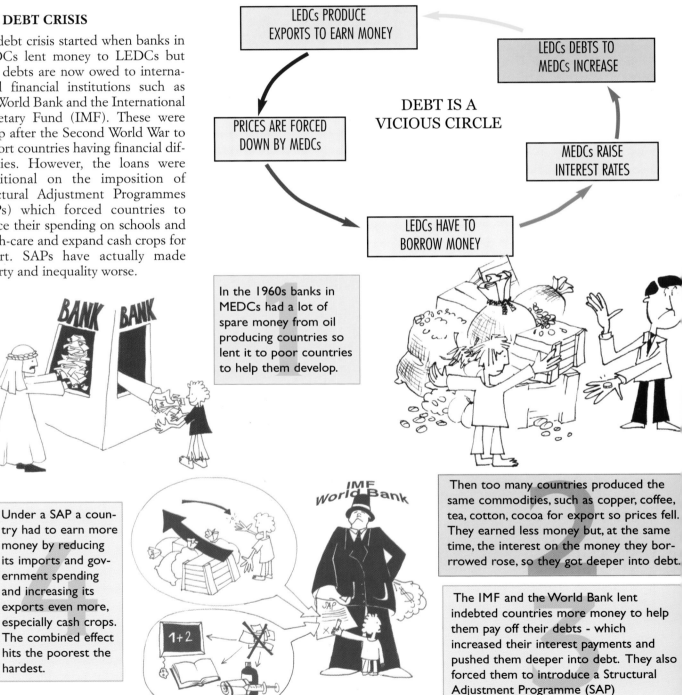

LEDCs PRODUCE EXPORTS TO EARN MONEY

PRICES ARE FORCED DOWN BY MEDCs

DEBT IS A VICIOUS CIRCLE

LEDCs DEBTS TO MEDCs INCREASE

MEDCs RAISE INTEREST RATES

LEDCs HAVE TO BORROW MONEY

In the 1960s banks in MEDCs had a lot of spare money from oil producing countries so lent it to poor countries to help them develop.

Under a SAP a country had to earn more money by reducing its imports and government spending and increasing its exports even more, especially cash crops. The combined effect hits the poorest the hardest.

Then too many countries produced the same commodities, such as copper, coffee, tea, cotton, cocoa for export so prices fell. They earned less money but, at the same time, the interest on the money they borrowed rose, so they got deeper into debt.

The IMF and the World Bank lent indebted countries more money to help them pay off their debts - which increased their interest payments and pushed them deeper into debt. They also forced them to introduce a Structural Adjustment Programme (SAP)

For every £1 LEDCs receive in aid from MEDCs, they give back £3 in debt repayment.
Illustration by Idir Kerkouche, 24, Algeria

"I was so proud of the achievement of the Live Aid concert. We raised US$200 million. Then I learned that Africa spends US$200 million every week repaying its debts to the West. That made no sense to me. It means that for every pound Western governments give to the poorest nations, the poor nations pay back THREE pounds to the West! Is that not barbaric? Is it not barbaric that Tanzania spends more on repaying its loans than it does on health care and education combined?"

Bono, U2,
speaking at the United Nations

THE EFFECTS OF DEBT

Many countries are now stuck in a cycle of borrowing from which there is no escape. Over 100 countries have experienced serious economic decline over the past three decades. In some countries, such as Nigeria and Indonesia, this is a result of debts run up by corrupt leaders. Today's governments still have to pay them off, depriving their poor citizens of health and education services.

QUESTIONS & ACTIVITIES

1 Why is the debt crisis similar to the slave trade? (2)
2 What are the structural adjustment programmes and why do poor countries dislike them so much?(4)
3 Explain why so many LEDCs have got stuck in a vicious cycle of debt. (4)
4 Draw up a table listing all the reasons for cancelling the unpayable debt of poor countries and all the reasons for not cancelling it. (6)
5 Why does debt kill thousands of people? (4)
6 Why do you think that, as the law currently stands, countries are not allowed to apply for bankruptcy but individuals are?(4)

I had never heard about the debt crisis until I went to a meeting about Jubilee 2000. Jubilee 2000 is a coalition of groups working in over 100 countries worldwide. Its goal was originally to cancel the unpayable debts of the world's poorest countries by the end of the year 2000. Now it is campaigning for a fairer international economic system. It is supported by a wide range of people such as Archbishop Desmond Tutu, Bono from U2 and the boxer Mohammed Ali.

The debt crisis is very complicated but the more I learned about it the more I realised that it is one of the most important factors affecting human development today. Debt is the cause of a number of problems including environmental damage, armed conflict, the drugs trade, migration and crippling poverty in most of the poorest countries of the world.

Many people argue that since these countries signed contracts for their loans, they should be made to pay them back. However, in many cases they have paid back the original loan several times over and are now paying off the interest. Also, those who made the loans should take some responsibility for giving money to sometimes corrupt, sometimes incompetent, governments.

If individuals run up too much debt and are unable to repay their loans, they are declared bankrupt and their debts are cancelled. At the moment countries cannot

JUBILEE 2000
A debt-free start for a billion people

declare themselves bankrupt so Jubilee 2000 is calling for the introduction of an internationally recognised bankruptcy law and tighter controls on both lending and borrowing to prevent such a crisis occurring again.

The Jubilee 2000 campaign has succeeded in cancelling or rescheduling a large amount of poor countries' debt. However, it is still not enough and the process is too slow. I became involved in the Jubilee 2000 campaign because I would like people in a few years time to look back on the debt crisis in the way we now look back on the slave trade. If it was possible to abolish the slave trade, even though many people accepted it as a normal part of life, then it should be equally possible for us to abolish the slavery of third world debt.

Heather Stabler, 22, UK

Jubilee 2000 campaigners in Köln, Germany.

Trading Together

Alongside the rapid march of globalisation, countries throughout the world have been grouping themselves in large, regional trading blocs. Regional groups can complement the global trading arrangements, helping to reduce disparities among countries and protecting them against the worst shocks of the global markets. (HDR 1992, p68)

WHAT ARE TRADING BLOCS?

Most people have heard of the European Union but there are many other regional trading groups all over the world - MERCOSUR, ASEAN or CARICOM. Such associations are a good idea because they can focus specifically on regional economic and ecological challenges.

Although there is a danger that powerful countries might become more powerful by expanding their regional influence, in practice, this does not seem to have happened. In the EU, poorer countries like Ireland and Portugal have benefited a great deal from subsidies funded by the rich members and intra-regional trade has expanded rapidly, benefiting all countries involved.

FREEING TRADE

The World Trade Organisation (WTO), created in 1995, was set up specifically to help reduce trade barriers, such as tariffs and quotas, between its more than 140 member countries. Having one set of trade rules for all is far simpler than having a different tariff in every country but there are also some drawbacks to unifying the system. When countries go to the WTO negotiations, they often work in their trading blocs in order to have more negotiating power. The problem is that then the most powerful countries tend to dominate the negotiations, leaving small or poor countries with little voice to change rules that may harm them.

The world is made up of many regional trading blocs and economic organisations.

NORTH AMERICAN FREE TRADE AGREEMENT (NAFTA)
This is the world's largest economic group but the USA and Canada benefit more from free trade within the region than Mexico, the poorest member.

CARIBBEAN COMMUNITY AND COMMON MARKET GROUP (CARICOM)
This group aims to create an integrated economic Caribbean market. Its members also work together on issues of foreign policy, health and education.

MERCOSUR
Since it was set up in 1991, the South American Common Market has increased trade between the four member countries sixfold.

THE EUROPEAN UNION (EU)
The EU is both a social and economic organisation. There are no barriers to the free movement of people, goods and money between member states. They also co-operate on issues like social and monetary policy, crime and human rights.

WEST AFRICAN ECONOMIC AND MONETARY UNION (UEMOA)
An organisation formed to promote co-operation in economic affairs.

OTHER ECONOMIC ORGANISATIONS

The Group of Eight (G8)

An elite group of the richest and most powerful countries in the world - Canada, France, Germany, Italy, Japan, Russia, the United Kingdom and the USA. Their leaders meet annually to harmonise policies and promote their interests.

The Group of Seventy-Seven(G77)

A group of what is actually now more than seventy-seven countries, led by India and Nigeria. It represents LEDCs collectively at international meetings, giving them a greater chance of being heard.

Organisation for Economic Co-operation and Development (OECD)

An association of thirty of the most powerful countries which protects the social and economic interests of its members and researches on these issues.

The Commonwealth

Former British colonies which continue to have informal trading links. They work to promote good governance, and take part in sporting, educational and cultural activities as well as development projects together.

ENVIRONMENT, SOCIAL & CULTURAL DEVELOPMENT

People Power In Seattle

In October 1999 demonstrations were held at the WTO meeting in Seattle to protest at its unfair trade policies. The protests succeeded in almost closing down the meeting and raising doubts around our current trade system.

"Our march advances into rush hour traffic. The Convention Centre is soon surrounded and trade delegates are blocked outside. Two hours are spent sitting, with arms linked, riot police forming a double line in front of us. We turn back many delegates. Later we learn that most of the morning sessions were cancelled. In the afternoon, meetings set for 200 people were attended by only 25!"

Jonathan Robinson, 22, UK

ASIA-PACIFIC ECONOMIC CO-OPERATION (APEC)

An organisation of countries in the Pacific Ocean which aims to reduce trade barriers between its members and promote external investment in the region.

SOUTH ASIAN ASSOCIATION FOR REGIONAL CO-OPERATION (SAARC)

This was set up to promote social and economic development, including issues such as environment, tourism, agriculture, education, health and technology.

ASSOCIATION OF SOUTH EAST ASIAN NATIONS (ASEAN)

Members work together to reduce trade barriers and build social and cultural bonds to enhance regional security and encourage the exchange of ideas.

ORGANISATION OF PETROLEUM EXPORTING COUNTRIES (OPEC)

A group of countries which rely on oil as their main export and work together to control production arrangements and world oil prices.

QUESTIONS & ACTIVITIES

1 a What are the most obvious benefits of trading blocs? (3)

b Can you suggest any problems with being a member of a trading bloc? (3)

2 a Which countries are currently left out of the major regional groupings? Why do you think this is? (5)

3 a What is the WTO? (2)

b Why did people want to protest about the WTO in Seattle? (4)

c How might an individual protest at the way world trade operates? (3)

8 Human Rights

From Charity To Justice

"All human beings are born free and equal in dignity and rights. They are endowed with reason and conscience and should act towards one another in a spirit of brotherhood".

Article 1 of the Universal Declaration of Human Rights, 1948.

WHAT ARE RIGHTS?

Human rights are the claims that every human being has on the way that society is organised and run. Their source comes from our shared moral beliefs that all people, regardless of race, gender or ability are born equal and should be given fair opportunities in life. Rights are extremely powerful because they transform appeals to charity into calls for justice.

Philosophers have argued about the importance of human rights for many centuries but it was only in 1948 when the Universal Declaration of Human Rights (UDHR) was drawn up and signed by 150 countries that human rights finally got widespread international recognition and agreement.

Today there are six major international treaties on human rights that all governments are encouraged to sign and turn into national law. These treaties cover issues such as torture, labour exploitation, health and education, women's and children's interests, racial discrimination, freedom of speech and political parties.

REALISING RIGHTS

Many governments, both in MEDCs and LEDCs, have signed all these human rights treaties but then have

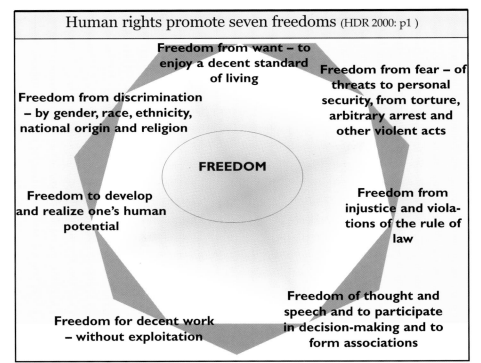

Human rights promote seven freedoms (HDR 2000: p1)

Freedom from want – to enjoy a decent standard of living

Freedom from fear – of threats to personal security, from torture, arbitrary arrest and other violent acts

Freedom from discrimination – by gender, race, ethnicity, national origin and religion

FREEDOM

Freedom to develop and realize one's human potential

Freedom from injustice and violations of the rule of law

Freedom for decent work – without exploitation

Freedom of thought and speech and to participate in decision-making and to form associations

failed to turn their noble commitments into national law and better policies. Once people learn about these treaties, however, they feel empowered to demand change and claim their rights. One way of drawing attention to human rights is collecting data to show how and why they are being neglected.

It is harder for LEDCs to realise rights because they often require money.

Ensuring the right to a fair trial, for example, means training judges and also paying them enough to prevent bribery. Although governments have special responsibilities because they create laws and shape policies, the rest of us have responsibilities too. In our local communities and also as members of the international community, we must stand up for rights and demand policies that respect and protect them.

Case Study

Myanmar

Myanmar (formally called Burma) is a country in South East Asia with a troubled political history. It has suffered internal strife from a long line of dictators, rebels and guerilla fighters. The citizens of Myanmar live in a permanent state of instability and fear.

In 1990, democratic elections were held. However, the military regime refused to accept the result of the election. They prevented the elected government from taking office and imprisoned its leader, Nobel Peace Prize Winner, Aung San Suu Kyi.

MYANMAR (BURMA)
Capital: Yangon
Area: 676,577 sq km
Population: 46,527,000

The Moustache Brothers In Myanmar

We stood in front of the house, hesitating. Was it the right address? It looked like all the other houses, as quiet and sleepy. Suddenly a man with a moustache and a big smile appears in the door and invites us in. Once inside, we have no doubts anymore. The room is crowded with objects, posters, photographs of all sorts which bear witness to the glory days of the Moustache Brothers.

Once we all have a cup of tea in our hands and are comfortably installed, the man begins to tell us the story of himself and his brothers. Still smiling, but with a very quiet voice, he tells us how popular their troupe used to be, the great and colourful traditional spectacles of dance, music and comedy they used to play through the country. Then he tells us how they began to have more and more trouble with the military government - because they were talking too freely, because they were friends of the democratic opposition leader, Aung San Suu Kyi. One of the brothers was sent to jail, soon followed by another one; they are still kept there, in terrible conditions. The government banned the show, but the rest of the brothers kept on performing it, obstinately, for a long time.

Now the pressure has become so strong that they have to hide. The show that used to be on the street is now inside, in a dark room in the back of the house. The crowd that used to come and see them is now limited to a small group, asked to be quiet and not to applaud. The dancers, surprisingly smiley, are moving gracefully in a deadly silence...

Text and photograph by Caroline Dalcq, 24, Belgium

Racial Discrimination in Education in Apartheid South Africa
(HDR 2000: p 97)

EXPENDITURE PER STUDENT, 1991 US$ THOUSANDS

WHITE 4
INDIAN
COLOURED
2
AFRICAN
1
0

PERCENTAGE OF ADULTS WITH AT LEAST 7 YEARS OF SCHOOL

WHITE 100
INDIAN 80
COLOURED 60
AFRICAN
40
20
0

QUESTIONS & ACTIVITIES

1 What is a right? How is it different from a wish? (4)
2 Research a country other than Myanmar where people have had some of their human rights taken away. Why did this happen? What can you do about it? (10)
3 Find and read the UDHR. Are all these rights realised in your country? Which ones need to be improved? (6)
4 Investigate how the human rights organisation Amnesty International works. Why does it have such a powerful international reputation? (8)

Good Governance

Governance is the process by which a society is managed and looked after. Good governance is when that process is handled honestly and efficiently for the benefit of all citizens, respecting and promoting human rights and human development. Freely elected governments, with clearly defined roles and responsibilities, are the best way to achieve it.

GOVERNMENT SPENDING

Many governments ignore their poorest citizens and do not focus on the right priorities. To advance human development, they need to increase social spending - the amount of money spent on health, education and welfare rather than the military, policing or ministers' salaries. Within the social services, priority should be given to primary education, not universities which mainly benefit those from higher income groups. Similarly, health spending should be focused on basic rural health care, rather than high-tech hospitals for the rich.

"Democratic regimes are the most likely to encourage popular participation." (HDR 1993: p78)

DEMOCRACY

Although no system of government is perfect, democracy incorporates most of the requirements for good governance such as equality, participation and representation. It allows citizens of a country to elect their leaders in regular, free and fair elections. Currently, it is the most common form of governance worldwide.

Repressive regimes often claim that economic growth and progress are only possible under a firm government. However, the more removed a government is from its people the less able it is to serve their needs and interests properly. As the 1991 HDR points out, "People must be at the centre of development. It has to be development of the people, by the people, for the people." (HDR 1991: p13).

Democracy is more than just winning votes at elections. Politicians can say anything to get elected without including people in the decisions or bringing any benefits to their lives

Illustration by Germán Kemerer, 15 & Ariel Avellaneda, 15, Argentina

POLITICAL PARTICIPATION

"Decentralising government from capital cities to regions, towns and villages can be one of the best means of promoting participation and efficiency." (HDR 1993, p66)

True political participation and democracy is more than just an election every few years. What is needed is diverse political parties and a strong civil society with pressure groups representing different sections of society and campaigning on different issues. More governments now allow these to flourish freely, and, through their energy and ideas, civil society groups are forcing governments to shift their priorities and improve their efficiency.

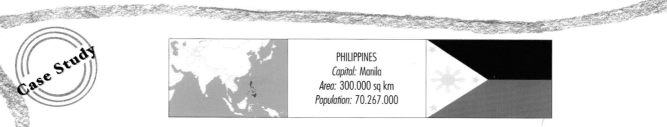

PHILIPPINES
Capital: Manila
Area: 300.000 sq km
Population: 70.267.000

Challenges For The Philippine Government In The Third Millennium

Over the last few centuries, the government of the Philippines has gone from aboriginal governance, to a monarchy, to various forms of colonial governance under the Spanish, Japanese and Americans, to what we have now: a democracy. Our government faces many of the same challenges as other governments around the world - the challenge of good governance.

Government officials like saying in interviews that the Philippines is a modern, progressive and highly industrialised country, but it is not! For example, with the oil price increase, buses and taxis had to raise their fares. Some people were furious and boycotted them so then the drivers reacted angrily and went on strike. The press published sensational stories, the politicians wondered what they could do, which was nothing, and Filipinos resorted to our national pastime of telling jokes about hopeless politicians!

Another huge problem is drugs. The government has to get rid of the 'head of the octopus' (the drug lords). Drug addiction cannot be stopped by cutting only 'tentacles'. The problem is that the drug lords are the politicians' friends. They pay them good money in taxes, and also give them bribes, so governments have no will to get rid of them.

Good governments must be willing and eager to listen to the cries of the poor masses. Every avenue must be explored to raise them out of poverty to be contented, productive, tax-paying members of society. Poverty costs governments money whereas peace and prosperity feeds money into governments, enabling them to invest in infrastructure and services, and save the environment. Surely, therefore, the goal of every good government is peace, prosperity and an end to poverty.

Fhilcar C. Faunillan, 15, The Philippines

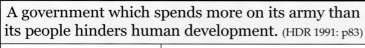

A government which spends more on its army than its people hinders human development. (HDR 1991: p83)

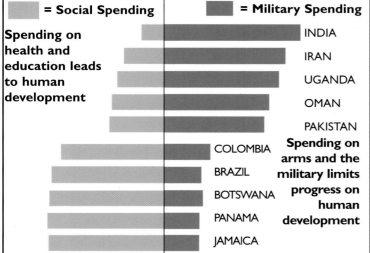

The 20:20 Compact On Human Development

In 1995 the United Nations held a 'social summit' in Copenhagen to discuss obstacles to human development and come up with solutions. Perhaps the cleverest idea was the 20:20 compact. A compact is a promise and the development experts wanted LEDC governments to promise that they would spend at least 20% of their budgets on basic services - health care, clean water, education, shelter, food - for the poorest people. In return, donor MEDC countries would promise to give at least 20% of their overseas aid to the same purpose. If the 20:20 compact were to be implemented over 10 years it would provide the funds needed to wipe out extreme poverty. It would help slow population growth, reduce environmental damage and create a healthy, productive workforce. However, like many good ideas, it has been shelved by governments.

(HDR 1996: p73)

Public projects, like road building programmes, schools or health programmes are much more likely to be successful if the communities they intend to serve have been involved in their planning. Also local political representatives can be more easily held responsible and be open to public scrutiny than national politicians.

QUESTIONS & ACTIVITIES

1 What is the main problem with government spending in many countries? (4)
2 Why is decentralised democratic government good for human development? (5)
3 Explain the 20:20 compact in your own words. How should it work? (4)

4 Design an election poster or a TV or radio advert for an imaginary British politician's campaign. (3)
5 Write a short report explaining why you chose the issues you did and which policies you think are more important than others. (10)

Corruption

The HDRs define corruption as, 'the use of one's position for illegitimate private gain'. It can be found in every country in different forms and occurs among political leaders, in government bureaucracies, in the military, in transnational corporations and in international banking. It is the second biggest obstacle to poverty eradication and human development after war.

CORRUPTION OCCURS AT ALL LEVELS OF SOCIETY

Corruption is most dramatic when it involves those at the highest levels of government, or rich and powerful figures. President Marcos of the Philippines is accused of taking $3 billion dollars of public money, putting it in a Swiss bank account and using it to buy property. Other corrupt leaders such as Idi Amin in Uganda or Mobuto Sese Seko in the Democratic Republic of the Congo (formerly Zaïre) used their position to amass huge personal fortunes worth billions of dollars while their own people lived in extreme poverty and their countries fell into ruins. Often they took foreign loans which their people now have to give back as debt repayments.

It is important to realise, however, that the problem of corruption is not just restricted to LEDCs or strict political regimes. Even MEDCs with well established democracies have scandals too. For example, in Britain there were 'cash for questions' scandals where people paid politicians money to ask particular questions for them in Parliament. It was also a shady financial scandal that ruined German Chancellor Kohl's reputation.

Corruption at the top seeps down to every level of society. In most big bureaucracies, small-scale corruption is widespread, especially where roles and lines of authority are unclear and if government officials are rarely supervised or monitored. In many LEDCs, officials demand a bribe for every form they sign, every licence

Corruption - Ignoring the responsibilities of power
Illustration by Idir Kerkouche, 24, Algeria and Chaffika Affaq, 22, Morocco

they issue or every benefit they distribute. Teachers demand bribes from students for good exam results. Once corruption is embedded in a society it is very hard to eliminate.

AN OBSTACLE TO HUMAN DEVELOPMENT

Corruption hinders human development because it undermines trust. If people don't trust their own leaders, they won't want to participate in civil society or contribute to human development. Corruption also reduces the amount of money a government can spend on its people. It diverts resources from the poor to those who can afford to pay bribes or use their

political influence to gain preferential treatment. Often important political decisions are bought by the biggest bribe, not what contributes most to the eradication of poverty.

THE SOLUTIONS

The main way to overcome corruption is to promote open, transparent government with a free press and a strong, independent judiciary intent on prosecuting wrong-doers. Another solution is to raise the salaries of those who are paid so little that they need to ask for bribes to feed their families. In Uganda the government managed to stop teachers selling grades and fixing test results by tripling their salaries.

However, corruption is increasingly being recognised as an international problem requiring international action and solutions. In 1993, a new organisation called Transparency International was launched. Its aims was to research and publicise cases of corruption in the same way Amnesty International investigates and exposes human rights abuses.

In all cases of corruption everyone involved should be held responsible because there are always two sides: those who offer bribes and those who take them. An impartial international organisation investigating all serious allegations of bribery and exposing those found guilty may help deter many tempted to corruption. Still, a large number of people consider paying bribes not only an acceptable but a necessary way to do business. It is this attitude which needs to be overcome in order for corruption to be reduced.

Bribery occurs to different degrees in societies all over the world.

GHANA
Capital: Accra
Area: 238.533 sq km
Population: 17.959.000

Pay Your Way

In Ghana words like 'embezzlement', 'fraud', 'bribe' and 'scandal' fill our newspaper headlines almost every day. This level of corruption has affected the spirit of patriotism in Ghana so badly that now nobody seems to have the good of the nation at heart any more.

Corruption determines who gets government contracts because officials take a bribe before signing any document or licence. People give bribes to get a job, and promotion is dependent on bribing the senior managers.

Traffic police responsible for checking lawlessness have become coin boxes. Drivers simply drop in any meagre amount of money when they are stopped for an offence, no matter how serious. People arrested for committing grievous offences that undermine the development of society and the national economy are left unpunished because of their position and financial status.

Schools are also corrupt and admission to education institutions can be a paid-for privilege for the well-connected and rich, not a result of academic achievement.

Mortuary attendants are demanding bribes before accepting the dead. Perhaps the only thing that Ghanaians have not been able to bribe is death itself! I am sure that if Ghanaians could control the source of the air we breathe they would take bribes before giving out the supply!

Randolph Amenudzi, Ghana

QUESTIONS & ACTIVITIES

1 What is corruption? (2)
2 How does corruption hinder human development? (5)
3 What strategies can be implemented to fight corruption effectively? (3)
4 Choose a corruption scandal which took place either in your own country or abroad. List the facts as they are known then describe ways in which the scandal could have been prevented. (10)
5 Do you think Transparency International is a good idea? Why or why not? What are the alternative solutions? (6)
6 a Read Randolph Amenudzi's article about corruption in Ghana *(left)*. What do you understand by the terms *fraud, embezzlement, scandal* and *bribe*? (8)
  b Imagine you are the person who is responsible for tackling corruption in Ghana. What methods would you use to combat the problem? (6)

Women Have Rights Too

The HDI index does not reveal the very significant differences between the opportunities available to men and women. The Gender Empowerment Measure (GEM), introduced by the HDR in 1995, was designed to measure these differences and put gender issues right at the centre of development thinking.

WHY FOCUS ON WOMEN?

Over 70% of the 1.3 billion people living in absolute poverty are women. There are twice as many illiterate women as men and most children not in primary school are girls. The death rate for girls is higher and more women suffer from malnutrition and vitamin deficiencies because they often go without food. In South Asia, there are only 94 females to every 100 males. This is due to the early death of girl children through disease, undernourishment and sometimes female infanticide - the killing of girl babies.

Much of the work women do is unrecognised, unpaid and unvalued because it is done in the home and community rather than in paying jobs. Even working women also take care of their household which means that, in all countries, women work longer hours than men. The HDR calculates that if women were paid for all the unpaid work they do worldwide, they should be paid $11 trillion dollars.

ECONOMIC OPPORTUNITIES

Women's poverty is a direct result of their unequal access to economic opportunities. More women are unemployed than men. Despite an increase in educated women, the number in work has increased very little. Women are more likely to be in low-skill jobs with low wages, long hours and bad working conditions. In many cases women's wages are only 75% of men's. Although there are more women overall in professional positions, there are still very few in senior management.

POLITICAL VOICE

Although women make up half of the population, they hold only 10% of the seats in the world's parliaments and 6% of ministerial posts. In 55 countries worldwide, including LEDCs like Bhutan and Ethiopia and MEDCs like Greece and Singapore, women hold less than 5% of parliamentary seats. Throughout history only 21 women have ever been heads of state.

LEGAL RIGHTS

Nowhere is discrimination against women more obvious than in their legal rights. In many countries around the world women face discrimination in their right to marry, travel, divorce, acquire nationality, manage and get a job or inherit property. In some countries in the Middle East a woman needs her husband's permission to get a passport. In some countries in Latin

Women spend much more time than men in household activities such as farming, collecting fuel wood and fetching water.

Photograph by Benedetta Rossi, Niger

AFGHANISTAN
Capital: Kabul
Area: 652,225 sq km
Population: 20,141,000

Case Study

A Catastrophe For Women's Rights

I'm a 16-year-old refugee from Afghanistan. Under the Taliban regime, I saw many women discriminated against in different ways in my country. I think this inequality is one of the biggest reasons why human development in my country has almost stopped. During the years of Taliban rule, I experienced the worst things possible. I was not allowed to go to school. I had to cover all parts of my body including my face. I was not allowed to leave my house without a close male family member. I was not allowed to speak in public or to work. These laws were not only for me, they were set by the all-male Taliban for every woman in the country. The penalty for breaking these laws is death or dismembering. Every Friday there was a public stoning of women who break the Taliban rules.

By good luck, I managed to leave my country but my heart ached for women and girls I left behind facing the same problems. Some could not tolerate it any more and committed suicide. Many women collapsed into mental illness. Now, after the fall of the Taliban, there is hope again, but let us learn the lessons: if the women of a country are forced into illiteracy, they cannot educate future generations. If a society denies women their basic rights, that country cannot develop.

Zuhra Bahman, 16, Afghanistan

An Afghan woman, covered as the strict Islamic law requires.

Men's And Women's Work

The cover of the HDR 1995 shows the amount of work done in the world.

The green is men's work; the red is women's. The top half shows paid work; the bottom half unpaid.

It indicates that women do more than half the work yet two thirds of it is unpaid; men do less work but three-quarters of it is paid.

America, there is no law against a man killing his wife if she commits adultery. But if a woman kills her husband for adultery, she is prosecuted. Many countries have no laws to protect women from domestic violence. In some countries sexual harassment has only recently become a crime. In rape cases, a woman often has to prove her innocence, which involves intrusive investigation of her sex life.

WOMEN'S EMPOWERMENT

The 1995 HDR introduced an index called the Gender Empowerment Measure (GEM), to show women's involvement in political and professional life. This measures:

- Women's representation in parliament.
- Women's presence as managers and professionals in business.
- Women's earning power in the work force.

The Scandinavian countries – Norway, Iceland, Sweden, Denmark and Finland – come top of the GEM, with the best political and professional opportunities for women. The GEM reveals that money does not buy gender equality. Japan has a GNP per capita of $23,300 but women hold just 9% of parliamentary seats; in Venezuela, with $5,800 per capita, they hold 28%. In the UK, women hold 17% of parliamentary seats, account for 33% of administrators and managers and for 44% of professional and technical workers.

QUESTIONS & ACTIVITIES

1 a Why be concerned about women? (3)
  b List all the areas in which women are disadvantaged and suggest some ways in which these problems could be overcome. (6)

2 a Why do women get paid less than men for the work they do? (4)
  b Do you think women should be paid for housework? Why or why not? (4)

3 a What factors are measured to calculate GEM? (4)
  b How can GEM be used? (4)

4 a Look at the gender empowerment data for the UK. In which jobs do women make up the greatest percentage of the workforce? (2)
  b What policies could help increase that number? (8)

Promoting Gender Equality

"Human development, if not engendered, is endangered."(HDR 1995: p23) Equality of opportunity for women is an absolute necessity for human development and economic progress. All countries must empower women to participate in all aspects of economic, social and political decision-making and reward them equally for their work.

ELIMINATING STEREOTYPES

The most important way of overcoming gender inequality is through challenging the existing images of the sexes. We need to change current working patterns so that women can take part in paid employment and men share the responsibility of looking after their home and family. These changes have been easier to promote and incorporate in MEDCs than LEDCs because their economies and social services are more structured and established.

For many years paternity leave, as well as maternity leave, has been a feature of Scandinavian life. It is now being introduced in the UK, USA and Japan. Other policies which these countries have pursued include flexible working hours to allow women to choose the hours they work, and providing school lunches and day-care centres for busy parent-workers.

INCREASING OPPORTUNITIES

Significant improvements for women in LEDCs can be achieved by concentrating on three key areas:

● Education: The benefits of educating a woman extend well beyond the woman herself to include the woman's family and her entire community. It increases her ability to participate in society, improves her access to paid employment and enables her to improve her quality of life. Educated women not only have fewer children but these children are likely to be healthier and better educated themselves.

● Health: With access to primary health care and information on reproductive health, women have more control over both the number of children they would like to have as well as the space between them. Bearing and raising children is an enormous strain and health risk. Over 500,000 women die each year in childbirth while another 20 million are disabled due to a lack of health care or qualified midwives.

● Access to credit : Most of the world's poorest people are women, so it is very hard for them to get loans from banks. However, the success of microcredit organisations, such as the Grameen Bank in Bangladesh which lends money to rural, landless women, has shown that women can save, repay their loans on time, and invest in health, education and housing for their families. Small and informal financial services which are specially tailored to meet the needs of women with simple application procedures and a shared management scheme should be encouraged.

SETTING GOALS...

The most powerful international agreement on women's rights is the Convention on the Elimination of All Forms of Discrimination Against Women (CEDAW). This was formally adopted at the United Nations in 1979 and asserts the equality of

Housework needs to be shared between both men and women.

Photograph by Benedetta Rossi, Niger

Case Study

MOROCCO
Capital: Rabat
Area: 446,550 sq km
Population: 28,913,000

Morocco And Women

Morocco has always been thought of as a country that treated women badly. In 1995 when the Gender and Development HDR came out, female literacy was 27% compared to 54% for men. By 1999 that had improved to 42% for women and 55% for men. Under our new king, His Majesty Mohammed VI, new opportunities are opening up every day for women.

Women now form half the student body of the University of Rabat - an unthinkable ratio even ten years ago. Although Morocco is an Islamic country that honours its religious traditions, women are allowed to dress as they please and they are equal before the law.

Dalal El Kortobi, 19, Morocco

women in both public and private domains such as marriage, work and child care. It also recognises women's civil, political, economic and social rights. However, the problem is that only 139 of the 186 UN Member States have signed up to CEDAW. Many of these either reduced the commitments or refused to make any commitments so that they still do not legally recognise the principle of gender equality.

... AND ACHIEVING THEM

All the HDRs claim that empowering women to be full partners in development is very important in achieving sustainable human development. They suggest establishing a new international non-governmental organisation called World's Women Watch. This would educate women on their legal rights as well as provide a channel for them to campaign for their rights.

The most important thing to remember is that equality for women is not just a moral right but a practical necessity. After all, women do hold up half the sky. It has been shown that, if women are better educated, healthier and more politically active, they are more likely to pass these benefits on to their children. Therefore equality in all aspects of life is essential for overall human development.

Women's empowerment - compared to HDI ranking (HDR 2000: pp157-168)				
HDI RANK/COUNTRY	SEATS IN PARLIAMENT HELD BY WOMEN, AS % OF TOTAL	FEMALE MANAGERS AND ADMINSTRATION, AS % OF TOTAL	FEMALE TECHNICAL AND PROFESSIONAL WORKERS, AS % OF TOTAL	GEM RANK
1. Canada	23	37	52	8
2. Norway	36	51	59	1
10. United Kingdom	17	33	45	15
19. Italy	10	54	18	31
24. Singapore	4	21	42	38
31. Korea, Rep. of	4	5	32	63
50. Trinidad & Tobago	19	40	51	22
78. Ukraine	8	37	65	55
91. Ecuador	15	28	47	43
173. Niger	1	8	8	70

QUESTIONS & ACTIVITIES

1 In which three key areas can women's rights be improved? Suggest ways in which this could be achieved. (6)

2 Why is equality for women important for human development? (4)

3 Suggest reasons why certain countries have a higher GEM ranking than HDI ranking and vice versa. (6)

4 a Choose one of the countries mentioned on this page and collect some statistics on the position of women there. (5)
  b What do these statistics tell you? (5)

Human Security

What is Human Security?

Each of the HDRs has tried to broaden our understanding of security. The HDR 1999 lists seven aspects of security which need to be pursued for human development to occur: Economic Security, Food Security, Health Security, Personal Security, Environmental Security, Community and Cultural Security, and Political Security.

PERSONAL SECURITY

Physical and mental violence are the most terrifying threats to individual security. In countries all over the world people are subject to assault, rape, crime, domestic violence, industrial and traffic accidents, verbal abuse, or become addicted to drugs or alcohol. Such experiences can often have devastating psychological effects on individuals and their families and it is often women and children who are most at risk.

COMMUNITY AND CULTURAL SECURITY

Traditional forms of cultural expression, such as speaking your language, practising your religion, wearing your traditional dress, and learning your community's history, stories and songs, are very important for individuals to develop a sense of identity and a sense of community cohesion.

However, the process of globalisation means that many of the world's languages, traditions and cultures are under threat of extinction from other, more dominant cultures. Much traditional knowledge and wisdom about health and medicine has already been lost. Protecting this cultural diversity is as important as protecting biodiversity.

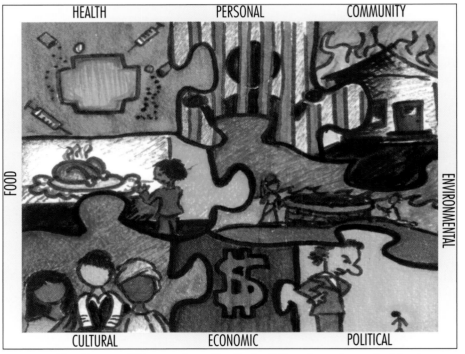

The Jigsaw of Human Security. Each of the pieces is needed for human security to be complete .

Illustration by Denise Smith, 13, Canada

ECONOMIC SECURITY

Everyone needs a basic income, from either a job or a social security system. However, jobs are often hard to find and keep, in both MEDCs and LEDCs, and especially for young people. For many of those who do have jobs, wage levels have fallen and it is ethnic minorities and women who are hardest hit. Governments are often unable to help. In MEDCs benefits have been cut whilst most LEDCs do not even have welfare systems. Some of the effects of such economic insecurity are poverty and homelessness.

POLITICAL SECURITY

All people should be able to live in a society which respects their basic human rights. The last few years of the

NEPAL
Capital: Kathmandu
Area: 140,797 sq km
Population: 23,340,000

Cultural Security In Nepal

We Nepalese are over-influenced by Western culture which is threatening our own culture. One day no other country will understand who the Nepalese people are. We will have no status in this new world.

English is clearly an important international language and it is good that people learn it, but why do people think that speaking Nepali is quite uncivilised? They want to forget it! We want to dress according to the fashion, but modern Western fashion crosses the limits of decency. Males prefer to grow long hair and wear earrings and females have short hair and wear short mini-dresses. This does nothing good to our country.

English and Hindi movies push Nepali movies out of the market. Music is dominated by pop, rap and jazz. Nepali songs are just not sold. We mostly read English comics and Nepali authors are being ignored. The most dangerous impact of Western culture is drug addiction. People use drugs as a fashion statement, to show off. Once they are addicted, they cannot quit.

My message is that we must preserve our own culture for coming generations and for the visitors when they come here, so that we can show them, "Look, this is our wonderful Nepali culture, inherited from our ancestors, preserved and enhanced for our children."

Joshu Pradhan, 13, Nepal

Fourth grade school girl in Ghana
"I shall feel secure when I know that I can walk the streets at night without being raped."

Woman in Paraguay
"I feel secure because I feel fulfilled and have confidence in myself. I also feel secure because God is great and watches over me."

Shoe-mender in Thailand
"When we have enough for the children to eat, we are happy and we feel secure."

Secondary school pupil in Mongolia
"Before, education in this country was totally free, but from this year every student has to pay. Now I do not feel very secure about finishing my studies."

HUMAN SECURITY - As People See It
(HDR 1994: p23)

Rural girl in Iran
"I believe that no girl can feel secure until she is married and has someone to depend on."

Man in Ecuador
"What makes me feel insecure above all is violence and delinquency, as well as insecurity with respect to the police."

last century brought much progress in this area as military dictatorships and one-party states were replaced by democracies and multi-party nations. Despite this, repression, arbitrary arrest and torture, police intimidation and control over the media are still common in many countries. These human rights violations are most common during times of political unrest.

QUESTIONS & ACTIVITIES

1 What are the seven elements of human security? Explain how the absence of one element can harm the others. (6)

2 a Put together a table listing the threats to cultural security in Nepal. (5)
  b Design some policies which could help protect the aspects of Nepali culture which are under threat. (4)

c Are there similar threats to cultural security in Britain? (4)
d What policies could be introduced to promote cultural security in Britain? (4)

3 Compile your own spider diagram of people's definitions of human security among people in your school or local community. (6)

Other Kinds Of Security

Health, environmental and food insecurity are the biggest threats to life. Each year disease, unsafe environments and poor nutrition kill many people. Environmental insecurity - pollution and degradation - can increase both food and health insecurity, which in turn poses new threats to the environment.

ENVIRONMENTAL SECURITY

The HDRs show that human security is threatened by environmental degradation at local, regional, national and international levels. Some environmental problems now have worldwide effects and therefore require global solutions.

Environmental threats to human security can be sudden and dramatic, like storms and landslides, or more long lasting, like air pollution or the greenhouse effect. However, even so-called 'natural disasters' are often caused by human beings. Deforestation has led to more droughts and floods and population pressures mean more people are living in areas previously considered dangerous and uninhabitable.

HEALTH SECURITY

The World Health Organisation defines health as, 'a state of physical, mental, emotional and social well being', and the HDRs identify it as a key component of human development. A healthy population is happier, more creative, more productive and more peaceful.

In LEDCs each year many people die from infectious and parasitic diseases, often caused by polluted water. In MEDCs the main causes of death are diseases of the circulatory system often linked with unhealthy diets and inactive lifestyles.

Governments and companies can provide health services such as hospitals, doctors and medicine, but each of us also has the responsibility to look after our own health. Education must include a health component to enable people to make informed decisions on how to protect their lives.

FOOD SECURITY

Food security means having both food available as well as the money to buy it. There is enough food produced in the world to feed everyone but the main problem is that it is not equally distributed. Some farmers in LEDCs face poor soils and droughts; others grow cash crops for export, such as tobacco, cotton and coffee, rather than growing food for their communities.

Food security is threatened by environmental degradation since soil erosion, deforestation, water pollution and overgrazing all affect the ability of land to grow food. This planet is going to have to feed 3 billion more people by 2050 - but each year 15 million acres are added to the 3.2 billion acres of desert. A turnaround in environmental management is therefore essential.

Replanting in the Abaleck Desert
Photograph by Ahmed Abdoulaye, 18, Niger

HIV And AIDS - A Global Epidemic

In many LEDCs the progress in human development of the last few decades is being wiped out by AIDS. Among adults, one in seven Kenyans, one in five South Africans and one in four Zimbabweans are living with HIV/AIDS - and these proportions are increasing. Worldwide, over 36 million people are living with HIV and AIDS, and about 15 million have died so far. In Africa alone there are an estimated 9 million AIDs orphans. The direct and indirect cost of the disease in the 1980s was around $240 billion worldwide. In a few years, it could be costing $500 billion a year - 2% of global GDP. Despite this, there are some countries where AIDS has yet to be acknowledged as a medical or development problem and where there is little knowledge or understanding about the ways in which the disease spreads and can be avoided. Education programmes and protection for sexual intercourse are essential but many LEDCs do not have the money to pay adequately for these.

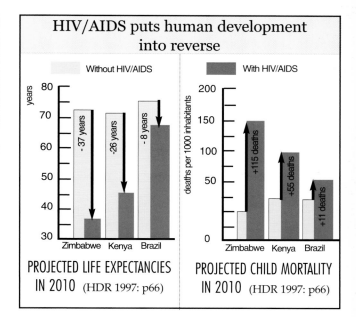

HIV/AIDS puts human development into reverse

PROJECTED LIFE EXPECTANCIES IN 2010 (HDR 1997: p66)

PROJECTED CHILD MORTALITY IN 2010 (HDR 1997: p66)

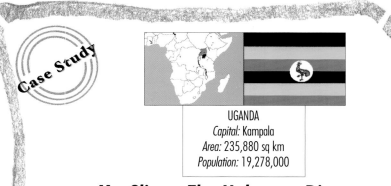

UGANDA
Capital: Kampala
Area: 235,880 sq km
Population: 19,278,000

Case Study

Mr. Slim - The Unknown Disease

More than two in every five adult deaths in Uganda are related to HIV/AIDS (HDR 1998: p35).

AIDS in Uganda was first recognised in the 1980s. It is thought the virus entered the country at trading towns along the border with Tanzania. At first people called the disease Mr. Slim, thinking that it was just a bewitching sickness on traders who had failed to pay debts abroad. Then people with medical knowledge - doctors and nurses - began to teach about the true causes of the disease.

Unsafe sex is one of the ways the virus spreads but here it happens a lot because many people are still ignorant. Taboo and social stigmas make it hard for people to discuss the disease with their partners. Women who do not have jobs may turn to prostitution, which spreads the virus even more. AIDS has set back the life expectancy here so that it is now less than fifty years.

The government is trying to educate people through television programmes, radio broadcasts and posters. However, there are many culturally engrained values and prejudices which still need to be overcome. It is everyone's duty to teach others about the causes of the disease and the impact it can have on your life.

Stephen Appollo Kalule, 17, Uganda

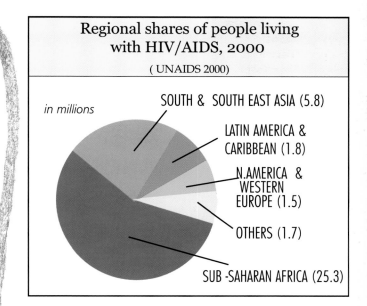

Regional shares of people living with HIV/AIDS, 2000

(UNAIDS 2000)

in millions

SOUTH & SOUTH EAST ASIA (5.8)

LATIN AMERICA & CARIBBEAN (1.8)

N.AMERICA & WESTERN EUROPE (1.5)

OTHERS (1.7)

SUB -SAHARAN AFRICA (25.3)

QUESTIONS & ACTIVITIES

1 a List four threats to environmental security. (4)

 b Why are natural disasters not always "natural"? (4)

2 What are the main causes of death for people in LEDCs and for people in MEDCs? (2)

3 How are health, environmental and food security inter-linked? (4)

4 a Which region of the world has the biggest share of people suffering from HIV/AIDS? (2)

 b Using information on this page and from the case study list the reasons why you think this is. (5)

 c What are the new projected life expectancies for 2010 and child mortality rates for people in Zimbabwe, Kenya and Brazil as a result of HIV/AIDS? (6)

 d How does HIV/AIDS affect human development? (5)

War and Peace

The battle for peace has to be won on two fronts. The first is the security front where victory spells freedom from fear. The second is the socio-economic front where victory means freedom from want. Only victory on both fronts can assure the world of peace.

The US Secretary of State speaking after the 1945 conference in San Francisco that created the United Nations (HDR 1994: p24).

MILITARY SECURITY

Security is traditionally seen as related to the military and as part of national defence plans. The United Nations (UN) was set up after the Second World War specifically to prevent more conflict but since then the number of wars has increased five-fold. The nature of wars has changed too: over 90% of them are civil wars (within countries) but the UN has no mandate to intervene. In 1900 5% of war casualties were civilian, whereas today about 90% are, many of them being children. Today about 100 million people worldwide are caught up in wars and 50 million people have lost their homes.

WAR AND HUMAN DEVELOPMENT

There is no doubt that warfare is a great threat to human development. A few minutes of aerial bombing or artillery fire can wipe out decades of painstaking development. For example, in Mozambique, war damage to primary schools denied two million children access to education. The East-West Cold War cost an estimated US$41 trillion.

The military can play an important role in protecting citizens from terrorism and international attack. That must, however, be set against urgent development priorities. Between 1983 and 1992, Afghanistan received more than US$600-worth of arms per person, despite the fact that it is a country desperately needing money for health and education.

It is not only war itself which causes problems. The disruption to food supplies and other services kills far more people than bullets. The preparations for war rob money from health and education budgets while the tanks and military exercises harm the environment. War employs people in industries which kill instead of improve lives.

War undermines standards of human development. Peace opens opportunities for human development.

Illustration by Mark Rechhulz, Austria

The Same Room

Afghanistan has been at war for generations. In 1979, it was invaded by the Soviet Union. Ten years of bitter fighting later, the Soviets withdrew leaving various leaders fighting for supremacy until the Taliban took control, shielding Bin Laden's Al-Qaeda network and financing itself through illegal sales of narcotics and repressing any dissent with brutal violence. The US-led war on terror displaced them in 2001. But any one under 21 in Afghanistan has known only war. It is their daily life.

We all have to stay in the same room because if we die, we want to be together. I'm not sure what may happen in the next minute. I wake up to the deep boom of an explosion. For a while, I can't figure out what is wrong, then bit by bit, I remember everything. It's war again.

Everyone is already awake. My father is smoking and has a gloomy look on his face. Everyone is very quiet. Time stands still. I can't detect any movement at all on anyone's faces. Now it's ten o'clock. The sound of artillery is coming nearer and nearer. Now I can hear the sounds of the weapons in pairs, once when they are fired and the other when they explode. I think about my future, my dreams, but everything seems impossible except death. I remember my friends, my school and my neighbours. I stand up, find a pile of letters from my bookshelf and read all that my friends have ever written to me. I know that I might not see some of them anymore. Maybe I'll die myself. I want to cry but I have to look brave.

Until the afternoon no one talks, no one eats. Then, by four o'clock, the fighting gets so near that we can hear the ordinary Kalashnikovs. It's even more horrible. My body starts shivering as I hear the shouting from my neighbour's house just down the road. They're near. Now I can hear my heart beat. I can't control myself. I want to shout. I want to run away. I wish it was a nightmare and I could suddenly wake up but this is reality and I have to face it.

It's time to go to the basement, the fighting has reached my own street. After a while sitting in the basement I hear the breaking of our windows. Then I hear somebody shouting loudly and saying to open the main door of our house otherwise they will set the house on fire. They beat my father and even my younger brother.

I can't do anything. They have the power of weapons. I wonder when this war will finish.

Zuhra Bahman, 16, Afghanistan

The biggest buyers of weapons among LEDCs 1998-1992 (HDR1994: p55)

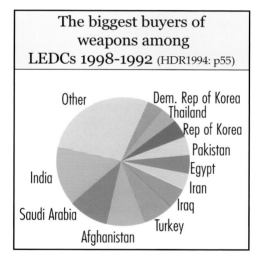

THE PROSPECTS FOR PEACE

Between 1987 and 1992, global military spending fell from US$995 to US$855 billion a year. However, while MEDCs reduced their budgets, many LEDCs maintained, and even increased, theirs. LEDCs could save over $10 billion a year by simply freezing their military expenditure at current levels. In 1948 Costa Rica abolished its military, immediately saving millions of dollars a year which it put into health care and education. It is now one of the most prosperous and peaceful Latin American nations with excellent relations with its neighbours.

So why do countries continue to spend so much on their military that it can harm, not enhance, human security? Armies can keep corrupt leaders in power and protect them from the anger of their citizens. During the Cold War some MEDC aid to LEDCs was given to countries specifically for their military just to make sure that they did not fall under communist control. However, the main reason for the continuation of the arms trade is that selling weapons is a profitable business. In order to bring about lasting peace the HDRs suggest regulating the arms industry and arms trade, expanding UN powers to intervene in civil conflicts and strengthening disarmament discussion forums.

The biggest suppliers of weapons to LEDCs 1988-1992 (HDR1994: p55)

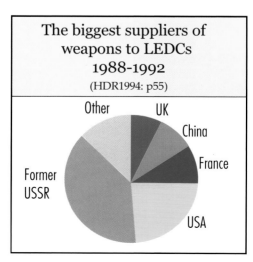

QUESTIONS & ACTIVITIES

1 What is military security? (2)
2 How do the preparations for war as well as war itself affect human development? (5)
3 a Put both the buyers and sellers of weapons in rank order with the biggest first. (4)
   b Which continent buys the most weapons? (2)
   c Choose three of the biggest buyers and find out what has been happening in those countries in recent years that may have been causing them to buy so many weapons. (10)
4 How did abolishing its army help Costa Rica? (4)
5 a Why do MEDCs sell so many weapons to LEDCs? (5)
   b Why might people in MEDCs oppose the complete abolition of the weapons trade and armies? (5)
6 Explain the reasons why some countries spend more money on the military rather than social services. (6)

The United Nations

We, the peoples of the United Nations, determined to save succeeding generations from the scourge of war, to reaffirm faith in fundamental human rights, in the dignity and the worth of the human person, and to promote social progress and better standards of life in larger freedom ...do hereby establish an international organisation to be known as the United Nations.
PREAMBLE to the UN Charter, signed on June 26th 1945, San Francisco

WHAT IS THE UNITED NATIONS?

The United Nations (UN) was set up in 1945 after one of the most violent centuries in history, featuring two world wars and scores of civil conflicts. The UN's tasks were to:

● secure global peace
● promote economic growth
● promote free trade.

THE UN AND HUMAN DEVELOPMENT

"The United Nations must serve the international community as its strongest human development pillar." (HDR 1994: p83)
Since 1945 the UN has been an important forum for bringing together governments to discuss and act on complex issues of common concern.

Many nations have welfare systems, ways to provide social services such as health care and education, benefits for the unemployed and pensions for the elderly. The HDRs suggest that the UN should act as a global safety net in the same way to meet the needs of the world's poorest. They see the UN as a potentially strong, responsible, and democratic form of global governance and make three recommendations about how to achieve this:
- strengthen the UN's role in achieving human development;
- create an Economic Security Council which would reflect the wider understanding of human security as defined in the HDRs;
- reorganise and strengthen existing global economic institutions.

STRENGTHENING THE UN

Among the many UN agencies are five focused on development which make up over 80% of its budget. Together they transfer about $5 billion a year to LEDCs, about 10% of total overseas development aid. The five agencies are:

• UN Development Programme (UNDP)
• UN Children's Fund (UNICEF)
• UN Population Fund (UNFPA)
• International Fund for Agricultural Development (IFAD)
• World Food Programme (WFP)

The UN thus has diverse institutions through which to channel resources to eradicate poverty. Over the years, the HDRs have suggested several ways to increase development funds, including the Tobin tax on currency exchange that could yield $150 billion a year; a tiny tax on Internet use; and an airline fuel tax. However, UN member states, led by the USA, have refused to contemplate any of them. The UN is not allowed to borrow money, let alone raise money through global taxes.

189 countries worldwide are members of the United Nations.

Chihiro Tanaka, 17, Japan

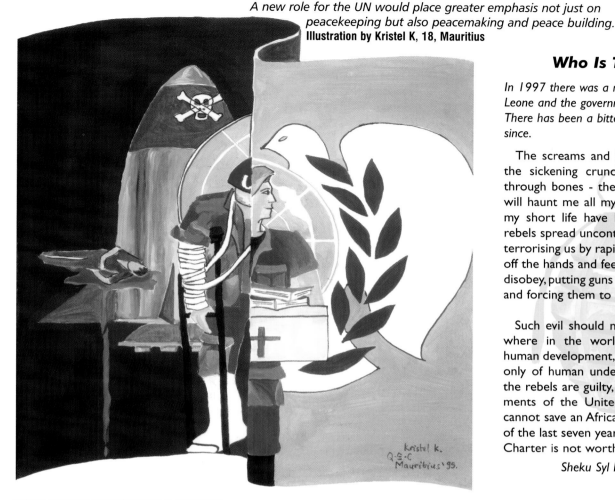

A new role for the UN would place greater emphasis not just on peacekeeping but also peacemaking and peace building.
Illustration by Kristel K, 18, Mauritius

Who Is To Blame?

In 1997 there was a military coup in Sierra Leone and the government was overthrown. There has been a bitter civil war there ever since.

The screams and howls of the women - the sickening crunch as machetes smash through bones - these are the sounds that will haunt me all my life. Three quarters of my short life have been lived in war. The rebels spread uncontrolled into our villages, terrorising us by raping our mothers, cutting off the hands and feet of those who dare to disobey, putting guns in the hands of children and forcing them to shoot their parents.

Such evil should not go unpunished anywhere in the world. You ask me about human development, my experience tells me only of human under-development. I know the rebels are guilty, but so are the governments of the United Nations. For if they cannot save an African child from the agony of the last seven years in Sierra Leone, their Charter is not worth a penny to me!

Sheku Syl Kamara, 21, Sierra Leone

ECONOMIC SECURITY COUNCIL

"An Economic Security Council can provide the high-level decision-making forum needed for human security." (HDR 1994: p84).

The UN Security Council is the main governing body of the UN. It is made up of fifteen member states. Five of these are permanent (UK, China, France, Russia and USA) while the other ten are elected every two years. The Security Council is responsible for dealing with conflicts and the use of peace-keeping forces.

The HDRs recommend that a new Economic Security Council is set up especially to deal with threats to peace and development from economic and social crises. The Council would raise funds for sustainable human development and work to ensure the well-being and security of every individual citizen and the environment.

OTHER INSTITUTIONS OF GLOBAL GOVERNANCE

Many of the structures for global governance and sustainable human development already exist, but a lack of governmental interest and a lack of resources has meant that they have not yet been very successful. They all need to be made more effective. For example, the World Bank should be responsible for helping economic growth in LEDCs in a way which incorporates social, political and environmental values. The World Trade Organisation needs to set out new, fairer trading rules and deal with disputes, while the creation of a new World Anti-Monopoly Authority could regulate the activities and policies of TNCs. Finally, even individuals, families, community groups and NGOs need to realise that they also have a role to play in promoting a global civil society.

QUESTIONS & ACTIVITIES

1 a What were the three tasks of the UN when it was set up? (3)

b What are the three ways in which the HDRs suggest that the UN could act as a global safety net? (6)

2 How could the existing institutions of global governance be strengthened to promote human development? (4)

3 Imagine you are helping to rewrite the UN's mandate for the 21st century. Write a short report outlining your vision for the organisation. (10)

4 a Research to find out what the UN does (use www.un.org if you have Internet access). Prepare either a newspaper article or a five-minute radio programme on the work of one of the UN agencies. (10)

b Find out what the UN has done since 1945. What do you think has been both its greatest achievement and its greatest failure and why? (10)

10 The Future

What Can You Do?

Each and every one of us has rights, but with those rights come responsibilities. Take ten years to get educated, take ten months to pressure governments to make a difference, take ten minutes to change the world today and every day through direct action. Enjoy your rights as a citizen of the world, but take your responsibilities seriously - our common future depends on it.

Start TODAY....
DIRECT ACTION

Every one of us must make the commitment to live our lives in a sustainable way. Governments can help with legislation and incentives but ultimately it is up to us.
Here are some ideas :
Use public transport
Use re-chargeable batteries
Buy organic products
Switch lights off when you leave a room
Close doors
Recycle as much as possible (aim for 80% of your total waste!)
Use energy saving light bulbs
Turn down heating rather than open a window
Improve home insulation
Use eco-friendly detergents
Take a canvas bag to the shops, refuse plastic bags or re-use old ones
Avoid plastic. It does not bio-degrade and lasts 500 years!
Never buy products which come from endangered species, such as ivory and coral
Compost all bio-degradable kitchen waste
Save water - use lo-flo shower heads and switch off

GET EDUCATED!

Education is vital for sustainable human development. Young people the world over are demanding meaningful education and access to knowledge on which they can base their decisions. We all have a responsibility to become aware of the issues of our day - the dangers of over-consumption, the threats to our environment, the unequal trading system. Once aware, we need to apply this knowledge and understanding to our daily lives. With education we can change ourselves, our communities and the future of the entire planet.

It is important for every member of society to have at least a minimum of education.

Governments have now committed themselves to providing universal primary education for all. 'Each One Teach One' schemes allow children who attend school to pass on learning to an 'apprentice' who is unable to go. If everyone in the world who could read did this for one other person, there would be no illiterate people left in the world.

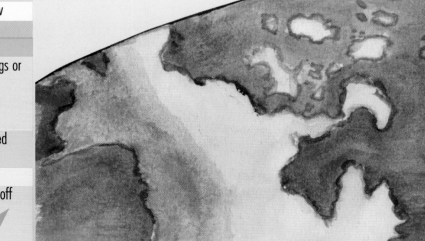

Some young people from MEDCs choose to spend a year in LEDCs as voluntary teachers. Teaching someone else to read and write is one of the most valuable gifts to give them.

MOBILISE AND MOTIVATE!

In a democracy we each have the right to stand up and state our concerns. In a free market we are each free to buy and sell within agreed rules and regulations. However, what is less often acknowledged is the responsibility which this places on each of us. Elected governments have to listen to public opinion. Manufacturers and traders have to listen to consumers. We, as individuals or as a group, can change how governments and businesses act.

Writing letters is a powerful medium for change. Send a letter to a government minister or business leader about an issue which concerns you. Send a copy to your local newspaper or even a national one. Every official letter is seen to represent the views of many people, so write that letter and make yourself heard. You could also join an organisation such as Amnesty International, Greenpeace or OXFAM and lend your support to their work. Make a donation, of time or money, and help to change the world.

As consumers we can 'vote' with our wallets. The boycotting of certain products and/or producers can pressure companies and manufacturers to bring about change. Royal Dutch Shell and Nestlé are two companies which have been boycotted in recent years because of their activities. Shell was boycotted because of their decision to dump the Brent Spar oil rig in the deep ocean. The boycott worked - Shell reversed their decision. Nestlé has been boycotted for many years because of its aggressive marketing of baby milk substitutes to women in LEDCs. Health professionals say they would be better feeding their babies breast milk as milk powders mixed with often-polluted water causes health problems for their babies.

Finally, think about where you want to focus your attention. Human development requires action on many fronts simultaneously but each person can only focus on a few areas. Choose what moves or inspires you most. Think what you are best able to do, and where you will have the most impact in your local area or in the world. Choose your cause and go for it! Every action, no matter how tiny, counts. Remember the goal: to get all local communities, nations and global society to embody the principles of sustainable human development. Remember this is not an end in itself. We will never wake up one day and be able to say, "We did it!" It is an on-going process which requires active commitment and involvement from all of us, every day of our lives.

dripping taps
Use solar energy
Take shorter showers
Plant trees! - Everyone should plant at least two trees per year as, on average, this is what each of us consumes per year
Don't drop litter
Practise sustainable tourism
Hand in books and clothes to charity stores
Buy products with a minimum of packaging
Mend your existing clothes
Only use a cupful of water when brushing your teeth
Water the garden in the evening when the sun is not at its hottest
Boil only the amount of water that you need
Do not buy aerosol products
Use unleaded petrol
Learn to use a computer
Be drug free and smoke free
Respect elders and children
Spend time with your family
Laugh at least once a day
Share what you have
Look after younger children
Smile at people
Give someone a hug
Learn another language
Volunteer
Take time to exercise and relax every day
Attend public meetings
Read your local newspaper
Give blood
Vote
Learn basic First Aid
Join a campaigning organisation
Write a letter to your Member of Parliament
Support local business by shopping locally
Fight prejudice and racism
Watch or read the news as often as you can
Lead by example!

ACT!

Visions Of The Future

Governments could pursue policies which lead to an upward spiral of human development for all. Unchanged policies, however, could result in a downward spiral to disaster.

Downward Spiral

Global consumption multiples 4-5 times

Population rises by 1 billion per decade

Average annual spending per person of richest 20%: US$55,000

Average annual spending per person of poorest 20%: US$2,000

Number of cars doubles to one billion

Rise in energy consumption

Sea levels rise

Small islands disappear

Extreme weather patterns

More droughts and floods

Increased water pollution

More fisheries collapse

Food shortages

Populations suffer water shortages

Women and children suffer worst

Small wars between states over resources

Increased global warming

Increased air pollution

Carbon emissions double

Loss of habitats and biodiversity

Deforestation

Increased water use

Human rights violations

Civil wars and internal revolutions

Wholesale war for world domination

MISERY, DESPAIR, ANARCHY

Illustrations by Idir Kerkouche, 24, Algeria

Upward Spiral

PROSPERITY, HAPPINESS AND MORE CHOICES FOR ALL

Implement global agreements on climate change, desertification and protection of common resources

Provide more opportunities for young entrepreneurs to generate their own employment

Find a vaccine to innoculate people against AIDS

Create a global fund to ensure food, shelter, healthcare, and education for all

Redistribute funds to lessen inequalities between the rich and the poor

Create a second chamber at the UN directly elected by civil society

Take steps to fight international crime

Strengthen the UN

Facilitate more technology transfer

Increase awareness of sustainable consumption

Promote sustainability certification and eco-labelling schemes

Ensure all children are educated about sustainable development

Ensure primary education for all

Promote cultural diversity through the global media and get everyone connected to the Internet

Promote democracy and strong judiciaries

Promote human rights

Use International Criminal Court

Create a Global Investment Trust to tax global commons

Strengthen civil society
Cancel unpayable debt

Increase ODA by at least $40 billion a year

Invest in renewable resources such as solar energy

Promote organic farming and conservation of the natural environment

Increase fines and taxes on polluting consumption patterns

Create green taxes to promote sustainable consumption

Remove all subsidies on damaging production processes

The HDR Covers

The graphics used on the cover of each Human Development Report 1990-1999 represent a different human development theme.

1990 - Introducing the HDI

The upper curve represents the ranking of nations according to the Human Development Index, while the lower curve shows their ranking according to GNP per capita. The two curves show that the differences between countries are greater in income rather than in human development. Also, there is no automatic link between a country's GNP and its level of human development.

1991 - Potential for Growth 1991

These three squares with their inset squares show how much money is actually devoted to human development by governments worldwide. The bottom square is national income with the inset showing the share spent by the government; the second shows government expenditure with the inset showing the share spent on social services; the third shows social expenditure with the inset showing the amount spent on human development priority areas such as primary health care and education.

1992 - Inequalities

The cover shows the global distribution of income (based on exchange rate converstions). The richest 20% of the population receives 82.7% of the total world income while the poorest 20% receives only 1.4%. The breakdown of global income is as follows:

WORLD POPULATION	RICHEST 20%	SECOND 20%	THIRD 20%	FOURTH 20%	POOREST 20%
WORLD INCOME	82.7%	11.7%	2.3%	1.9%	1.4%

1993 - Jobless Growth

This cover shows jobless growth in the world. The upper curve represents growth in GDP (between 1975-90 and the projections on to 2000) in the major regions - OECD coutries, Latin America, Sub-Saharan Africa, South Asia and East Asia. The lower curve represents growth in employment for the same regions. It shows that employment growth has seriously lagged behind economic growth.

1994 - Peace Dividend

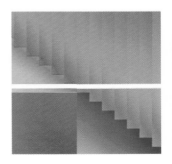

This graph shows the decline in global military spending between 1987-94, which has generated a US$935 billion 'peace dividend'. If global military spending were to continue to decline by 3% a year between 1995-2000, this would generate another $460 billion peace dividend which could be used for social services and promoting human development.

1995 - Gender & development

This graphic dramatically captures the undervaluation of women's work. The green is men's work, the red is women's. The top half shows paid work, the bottom half unpaid. It indicates:
- Of the total amount of work done in the world, women do more than half;
- Three-quarters of men's work is in paid activities; only one third of women's work is paid;
- As a result, men receive the majority of income and recognition for their economic contribution, while most of women's work remains unpaid, unrecognised and undervalued.

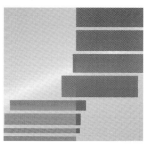

1996 - Income winners & losers

The diagram shows the regional shares of world population. The top four bars to the right of the central vertical line represents the 3 billion people in 60 countries where incomes have risen in the last decades. The bottom bars to the left represents the 1.5 billion in about 100 countries where incomes have fallen. The diagonal line in the background shows the slow but significant improvement in human development in almost all countries in recent decades.

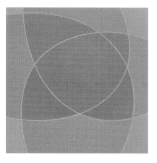

1997 - Dimensions of poverty

This cover shows the many dimensions of human poverty: each of the long curved lines represents one dimension of human deprivation: 1) short life; 2) illiteracy; 3) social exclusion; 4) lack of material means. These dimensions overlap, like a Venn Diagram.

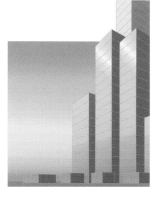

1998 - Consumption

The columns show ratios of consumption between the poorest and the richest of the world. The consumption levels of the 20% of people who live in the poorest countries are represented by the single blocks in the foreground. The relative consumption levels of the 20% who live in the richest countries are represented by the stacks of blocks behind. How much do all the richest countries consume compared to the poorest?

1. MEAT - 11 TIMES AS MUCH
2. ENERGY - 17 TIMES AS MUCH
3. OVERALL CONSUMPTION - 16 TIMES AS MUCH
4. FISH - 7 TIMES AS MUCH

5. TELEPHONE LINES - 49 TIMES AS MANY
6. PAPER - 77 TIMES AS MUCH
7. CARS - 145 TIMES AS MANY

1999 - Globalisation

The pie slices show the share of world population in different regions of the world. South Asia is the big slice at top left, sub-Saharan Africa below it to the left, the OECD countries to the right. The dark wedges show the proportion of Internet users in each region - a good indication of the number of people with access to the global community. The biggest wedge is in the OECD region - the world's richest countries. The other wedges show tiny numbers of Internet users in other regions where people are thus less able to take advantage of the benefits of globalisation.

Indicator Tables

Each Human Development Report, from 1990 to 2001, contains a long list of the indicators used t measure different aspects of human development in every country and rank them accordingly. Thes measurements and rankings provide one of the clearest pictures of human life in each country.

HDI Rank / Country	Life expectancy at birth (years) 1999	Adult literacy rate (% age 15 and above) 1999	Combined primary, secondary and terti- ary gross enrolment ratio (%) 1999	GDP per capita (PPP US$) 1999	Population 1999 millions	Population 2015 millions	Health Exp. (as% GDP) 1998	Education Exp. (as % GNP) 1995-7	Defence Exp. (as % GDP) 1999
1. Norway	78.4	-	97	28,433	4.4	4.7	7.4	7.7	2.2
2. Australia	78.8	-	116[1]	24,574	18.9	21.9	5.9	5.5	1.9
3. Canada	78.7	-	97[1]	26.251	30.5	34.4	6.3	6.9	1.3
4. Sweden	79.6	-	101	22,636	8.9	8.6	6.7	8.3	2.1
5. Belgium	78.2	-	109	25,443	10.2	10.3	7.9	3.1	1.4
6. United States of America	76.8	-	95	31,872	280.4	321.2	5.8	5.4	3.0
7. Iceland	79.1	-	89	27,835	0.3	0.3	7.2	4.0	0.0
8. Netherlands	78.0	-	102	24,215	15.8	16.4	6.0	6.0	1.8
9. Japan	80.8	-	82	24,898	126.8	127.5	5.9	5.3	1.0
10. Finland	77.4	-	103	23,096	5.2	5.2	5.2	8.1	1.2
11. Switzerland	78.8	-	84	27,171	7.0	-0.2	7.6	5.4	1.1
12. Luxembourg	77.2	-	73	42,769	0.4	0.5	5.4	4.8	0.8
13. France	78.4	-	94	22,897	59.0	61.9	7.3	6.0	2.7
14. United Kingdom	77.5	-	106	22.093	59.3	60.6	5.9	5.3	2.5
15. Denmark	76.1	-	97	25,869	5.3	5.4	6.7	8.1	1.6
16. Austria	77.9	-	90	25.089	8.1	7.8	5.8	5.4	0.9
17. Germany	77.6	-	94	23,742	82.0	80.7	7.9	4.8	1.5
18. Ireland	76.4	-	91	25,918	3.8	4.4	4.5	6.0	0.8
19. New Zealand	77.4	-	99	19.104	3.7	4.1	6.2	7.3	1.1
20. Italy	78.4	98.4	84	22,172	57.5	55..2	-5.6	4.9	2.0
21. Spain	78.3	97.6	95	18.079	39.0	39.0	5.4	5.0	1.3
22. Israel	78.6	95.8	83	18,440	5.9	7.7	6.0	7.6	8.1
23. Greece	78.1	97.1	81	15,414	10.6	10.5	-4.7	3.1	4.9
24. Hong Kong, China (SAR)	79.4	93.3	63	22,172	6.7	8.0	1.1	-	2.9
25. Cyprus	77.9	96.9	69	19.006	0.8	0.9	-	4.5	3.4
26. Singapore	77.4	92.1	75	20,767	3.9	4.8	1.2	3.0	5.3
27. Korea (Rep. of)	74.7	97.6	90	15,712	46.4	50.6	2.3	3.7	2.8
28. Portugal	75.5	91.9	96	16,064	10.0	10.0	5.2	5.8	2.2
29. Slovenia	75.3	99.6	83	15,977	2.0	1.9	6.6	5.7	1.4

HDI Rank / Country	Life expectancy at birth (years) 1999	Adult literacy rate (% age 15 and above) 1999	Combined primary, secondary and tertiary gross enrolment ratio (%) 1999	GDP per capita (PPP US$) 1999	Population 1999 millions	Population 2015 millions	Health Exp. (as% GDP) 1998	Education Exp. (as % GNP) 1995-7	Defence Exp. (as % GDP) 1999
30. Malta	77.9	91.8	80	15,189	0.4	0.4	-	5.1	0.8
31. Barbados	76.6	97.0	77	14,353	0.3	0.3	4.5	7.2	-
32. Brunei Darussalam	75.7	91.0	76	17,868	0.3	0.4	-	-	7.6
33. Czech Rep.	74.7	-	70	13,018	10.3	10.0	6.7	5.1	2.0
34. Argentina	73.2	96.7	83	12,277	36.6	43.5	4-9	3.5	1.5
35. Slovakia	73.1	-	76	10,591	5.4	5.4	5.7	4.7-	1.7
36. Hungary	71.1	99.3	81	11,430	10.0	9.3	5.2	4.6	1.4
37. Uruguay	74.2	-97.7	79	8,879	3.3	3.7	1.9-	3.3	1.2
38. Poland	73.1	99.7	84	8,450	3.2	3.5	4.7	7.5	2.0
39. Chile	75.2	95.6	78	8,652	15.0	17.9	2.7	3.6	3.1
40. Bahrain	73.1	87.1	80	13,688	0.6	0.8	2.6	4.4	5.0
41. Costa Rica	76.2	95.5	67	8.860	3.9	5.2.	5.2	5.4	-
42. Bahamas	69.2	95.7	74	15,258	0.3	0.4	2.5-	-	-
43. Kuwait	76.0	81.9	59	17,289	1.8	2.8	-	5.0	8.3
44. Estonia	70.3	98.0	86	8,355	1.4	1.2	–	7.2	1.4
45. United Arab Emirates	74.8	-75.1	68	18.162	2.6	3.2	0.8	1.7	3.2
46. Croatia	73.6	98.2	68	7,387	4.7	4.6	-	5.3	4.2
47. Lithuania	71.8	99.5	80	6,656	3.7	3.5	4.8	5.9	1.0
48. Qatar	69.3	80.8	75	18,789	0.6	0.7	-	3.4	-
49. Trinidad and Tobago	74.1	93.5	65	8,176	1.3	1.4	2.5	4.4	0.9
50. Lativa	70.1	99.8	82	6,264	2.4	2.2	4.2	6.5	0.9
51. Mexico	72.4	91.1	71	8,297	97.4	119.2	-	4.9	0.6-
52. Panama	73.9	91.7	74	5,875	2.8	3.5	4.9	5.1	1.4
53. Belarus	68.5	99.5	77	6,876	10.2	9.7	5.9	4.9	1.3
54. Belize	73.8	93.1	73	4,959	0.2	0.3	2.2	5.0	1.5
55. Russian Federation	66.1	99.5	78	7,473	146.2	133.3	-	3.5	3.8
56. Malaysia	72.2	87.0	66	8,209	21.8	27.9	1.4	4.9	2.3
57. Bulgaria	70.8	98.3	72	5.071	8.0	6.8	3.8	3.2	2.8
58. Romania	69.8	98.0	-69	6.041	22.5	21.4	-	3.6	1.6
59. Libyan Arab Jamahiriy	70.3	79.1	92	7,570	5.2	7.1	-	-	-
60. Macedonia, TFYR	73.0	94.0	70	4,651	2.0	2.1	5.5	5.1	2.5
61. Venezuala	72.7	92.3	65	5,495	23.7	30.9	2.6	5.2	1.4
62. Colombia	70.9	91.5	73	5,749	41.4	52.6	5.2	4.1	2.5
63. Mauritius	71.1	84.2	63	9,107	1.2	1.3	1.8	4.6	0.2
64. Suriname	70.4	93.0	83	4,178	0.4	0.4	-	3.5	-
65. Lebanon	72.9	85.6	78	4,705	3.4	4.2	2.2	2.5	3.6
66. Thailand	69.9	95.3	60	6,132	62.0	72.5	1.9	4.8	1.8
67. Fiji	68.8	92.6	84	4,799	0.8	0.9	2.9	-	1.6
68. Saudi Arabia	71.3	76.1	61	10,815	19.6	31.7	-	7.5	13.2

HDI Rank / Country	Life expectancy at birth (years) 1999	Adult literacy rate (% age 15 and above) 1999	Combined primary, secondary and tertiary gross enrolment ratio (%) 1999	GDP per capita (PPP US$) 1999	Population 1999 millions	Population 2015 millions	Health Exp. (as% GDP) 1998	Education Exp. (as % GNP) 1995-7	Defence Exp. (as % GDP) 1999
69. Brazil	67.5	84.9	80	7,037	168.2	201.4	2.9	5.1	1.3
70. Philippines	69.0	95.1	82	3,805	74.2	95.9	3.4	1.7	1.2
71. Oman	70.8	70.3	58	13,356	2.5	4.1	2.9	4.5	10.1
72. Armenia	72.7	98.3	80	2,215	3.8	3.8	3.1	2.0	3.6
73. Peru	68.5	89.6	80	4,622	25.2	31.9	2.4	2.9	-
74. Ukraine	68.1	99.6	27	3,458	50.0	43.3	3.6	5.6	3.1
75. Kazakhstan	64.4	99.0	77	4,951	16.3	16.0	3.5	4.4	0.9
76. Georgia	73.0	99.6	70	2,431	5.3	4.8	0.5	5.2	1.2
77. Maldives	66.1	96.2	77	4,423	0.3	0.5	5.1	6.4	-
78. Jamaica	75.1	86.4	62	3,561	2.6	3.0	3.2	7.5	-
79. Azerbaijan	71.3	97.0	71	2,850	8.0	8.7	-	3.0	2.6
80. Paraguay	69.9	93.0	64	4,384	5.4	7.8	1.7	4.0	1.1
81. Sri Lanka	71.9	91.4	70	3,279	18.7	21.5	1.4	3.4	3.6
82. Turkey	69.5	84.6	62	6,380	65.7	79.0	-	2.2	5.0
83. Turkmenistan	65.9	98.0	81	3,347	4.6	6.1	4.1	-	3.4
84. Ecuador	69.8	91.0	77	2,994	12.4	15.9	1.7	3.5	-
85. Albania	73.0	84.0	71	3,189	3.1	3.4	3.5	-	1.4
86. Dominican Republic	67.2	83.2	72	5,507	8.2	10.1	1.9	2.3	-
87. China	70.2	83.5	73	3,617	1,264.8	1,410.2	-	2.3	2.1
88. Jordan	70.1	89.2	55	3,955	4.8	7.2	5.3	7.9	10.0
89. Tunisia	69.9	69.9	74	5,957	9.4	11.3	2.2	7.7	1.7
90. Iran, Islamic Republic of	68.5	75.7	73	5,531	69.2	87.1	1.7	4.0	2.7
91. Cape Verde	69.4	73.6	77	4,490	0.4	0.6	1.8	-	0.9
92. Kyrgyzstan	67.4	97.0	68	2,573	4.8	5.8	2.9	5.3	1.7
93. Guyana	63.3	98.4	66	3,640	0.8	0.7	-4.5	5.0	-
94. South Africa	53.9	84.9	93	8,908	42.8	44.6	3.3	7.6	1.3
95. El Salvador	69.5	78.3	63	4,344	6.2	8.0	2.6	2.5	0.9
96. Samoa (Western)	68.9	80.2	65	4,047	0.2	0.2	4.8	-	-
97. Syrian Arab Republic	70.9	73.6	63	4,454	23.2	2.4	4.2	5.6	-
98. Moldova, Republic of	66.6	98.7	72	2,037	4.3	4.2	6.4	10.6	0.5
99. Uzbekistan	68.7	88.5	76	2,251	24.5	30.6	3.4	7.7	1.7
100. Algeria	69.3	66.6	72	5,063	29.8	38.0	2.6	5.1	3.8
101. Viet Nam	67.8	93.1	67	1,860	77.1	94.4	0.8	3.0	-
102. Indonesia	65.8	86.3	65	2,857	209.3	250.1	0.7	1.4	1.1
103. Tajikistan	67.4	99.1	67	1,031	6.0	7.1	5.2	2.2	1.4
104. Bolivia	62.0	85.0	70	2,355	8.1	11.2	4.1	4.9	1.8
105. Egypt	66.9	54.6	76	3,420	66.7	84.4	-	4.8	2.7
106. Nicaragua	68.1	68.2	63	2,279	4.9	7.2	8.3	3.9	1.1
107. Honduras	65.7	74.0	61	2,340	6.3	8.7	3.9	3.6	0.6

HDI Rank / Country	Life expectancy at birth (years) 1999	Adult literacy rate (% age 15 and above) 1999	Combined primary, secondary and tertiary gross enrolment ratio (%) 1999	GDP per capita (PPP US$) 1999	Population 1999 millions	Population 2015 millions	Health Exp. (as% GDP) 1998	Education Exp. (as % GNP) 1995-7	Defence Exp. (as % GDP) 1999
108. Guatemala	64.5	68.1	49	3,674	11-.1	16.3	2.1	1.7	0.6
109 Gabon	52.6	63.0	86	6.024	1.2	1.8	2.1	2.9	0.3
110. Equatorial Guinea	50.6	82.2	64	4,676	0.4	0.7	-	1.7	-
111. Namibia	44.9	81.4	78	5,468	1.7	2.3	4.1	9.1	3.6
112. Morocco	67.2	48.0	52	3,419	29.3	37.7	1.2	5.3	-
113. Swaziland	47.0	78.9	72	3,987	0.9	1.0	2.7	5.7	1.7
114. Botswana	41.9	76.4	70	6,872	1.5	1.7	2.5	8.6	3.4
115 India	62.9	56.5	56	2,248	992.7	1,230.5	-	3.2	2.4
116. Mongolia	62.5	62.3	58	1,711	2.5	3.1	-	5.7	2.1
117. Zimbabwe	42.9	88.0	65	2,876	12.4	16.4	-	7.1	3.3
118. Myanmar	56.0	84.4	55	1,027	47.1	55.3	0.2	1.8	0.8
119. Ghana	56.6	70.3	42	1,881	18.9	26.4	1.8	4.2	0.8
120. Lesotho	47.9	82.9	61	1,854	2.0	2.1	-	8.4	3.2
121. Cambodia	56.4	68.2	62	1,361	12.8	18.6	0.6	2.9	2.5
122. Papua New Guinea	56.2	63.9	39	2,367	4.7	6.6	2.5	-	1.0
123. Kenya	51.3	81.5	51	1,022	30.0	40.00	2.4	6.5	1.9
124. Comoros	59.4	59.2	36	1,429	0.7	1.1	-	-	-
125. Cameroon	50.0	74.8	43	1,573	14.6	20.2	1.0	-	1.5
126. Congo	51.1	79.5	63	727	2.9	4.7	2.0	6.1	-
127. Pakistan	59.6	45.0	40	1,834	137.0	204.3	0.9	2.7	4.4
128. Togo	51.6	56.3	62	1,410	4.4	6.6	1.3	4.5	-
129. Nepal	58.1	40.4	60	1,237	22.5	32.1	1.3	3.2	0.9
130. Bhutan	61.5	42.0	33	1,341	2.0	3.1	3.2	4.1	-
131. Lao People's Dem. Rep.	53.1	47.3	58	1,471	5.2	7.3	1.2	2.1	2.4
132. Bangladesh	58.9	40.8	37	1,483	134.6	183.2	1.7	2.2	1.6
133. Yemen	60.1	45.2	51	806	17.6	33.1	-	7.0	5.6
134 Haiti	52.4	48.8	52	1,464	8.0	10.2	1.4	-	-
135. Madagascar	52.2	65.7	44	799	15.5	24.1	1.1	1.9	1.4
136. Nigeria	51.5	62.6	45	853	110.8	165.3	0.8	0.7	1.4
137.Djibouti	44.0	63.4	22	2,377	0.6	0.7	-	-	4.4
138. Sudan	55.6	56.9	34	664	30.4	32.4	-	1.4	2.6
139. Mauritania	51.1	41.6	41	1,609	2.6	4.1	1.4	5.1	2.3
140. Tanzania, United Rep. of	51.1	74.7	32	501	34.3	49.3	1.3	-	1.3
141. Uganda	43.2	66.1	45	1,167	22.6	38.7	1.9	2.6	2.1
142 Congo, Dem. Rep. of the	51.0	60.3	32	801	49.6	84.0	-	-	-
143. Zambia	41.0	77.2	49	756	10.2	14.8	3.6	2.2	1.0
144 Cote d'Ivoire	47.8	45.7	38	1,654	15.7	21.5	1.2	5.0	0.9
145 Senegal	52.9	36.4	36	1,419	9.2	13.5	2.6	3.7	1.5
146. Angola	45.0	42.0	23	3,179	12.8	20.8	-	-	23.5

Indicator Tables

HDI Rank / Country	Life expectancy at birth (years) 1999	Adult literacy rate (% age 15 and above) 1999	Combined primary, secondary and tertiary gross enrolment ratio (%) 1999	GDP per capita (PPP US$) 1999	Population 1999 millions	Population 2015 millions	Health Exp. (as% GDP) 1998	Education Exp. (as % GNP) 1995-7	Defence Exp. (as % GDP) 1999
147. Benin	53.6	39.0	45	933	6.1	9.4	1.6	3.2	-
148. Eritrea	51.8	52.7	26	880	3.5	5.7	-	1.8	22.9
149 Gambia	45.9	35.7	45	1,580	1.3	1.8	1.9	4.9	0.8
150. Guinea	47.1	35.0	28	1,984	8.0	11.3	2.2	1.9	1.4
151. Malawi	40.3	59.2	73	586	11.0	15.7	2.8	5.4	0.8
152. Rwanda	39.9	65.8	40	885-	7.1	10.5	2.0	-	4.2
153. Mali	51.2	39.8	28	753	11.0	17.7	2.1	2.2	2.2
154. Central African Republic	44.3 45.4	24	1,166	3.6	4.9	2.0	-	-	
155. Chad	45.5	41.0	31	850	7.6	12.4	2.3	2.2	1.2
156. Guinea-Bissau	44.5	37.7	37	678	1.2	1.7	-	-	1.3
157. Mozambique	39.8	43.2	23-	861	17.9	23.5	2.8	-	2.4
158. Ethiopia	44.1	37.4	27	628	61.4	89.8	1.7	4.0	9.0
159. Burkina Faso	46.1	23.0	23	965	11.2	18.5	1.2	3.6	1.6
160. Burundi	40.6	46.9	19	578	6.3	9.8	0.6	4.0	6.1
161. Niger	44.8	15.3	16	753	10.5	18.5	1.2	2.3	-
162. Sierra Leone	38.3	32.0	27	448	4.3	7.1	0.9	-	1.6

Information taken from HDR 2001.

[1]There are two different HPI rankings which use different data The HPI-1 is used for LEDCs, while the HPI-2 (marked with [1]) is used for MEDCs. These two indexes cannot be used to measure the levels of poverty between MEDCs and LEDCs.

Measuring the HDI
The HDI measures the average achievements in a country in three basic dimensions of human development:
• A long and healthy life, as measured by life expectancy at birth.
• Knowledge, as measured by the adult literacy rate and the combined primary, secondary and tertiary gross enrolment rate.
• A decent standard of living, as measured by GDP per capita.

Measuring the GDI
• The GDI uses the same criteria as the HDI but adjusts the average achievement to reflect the inequalities between men and women.

Measuring the GEM
The GEM focuses on women's opportunities rather than their capabilities and measures gender inequality in three ways:
• Political participation and decision-making power, as measured by women's and men's percentage shares of parliamentary seats.
• Economic participation and decision making power, as measured by two indicators - women's and men's percentage shares of postions as legislators, senior officials and managers; and women's and men's percentage shares of professional and technical positions.
• Power over economic resources, as measured by women's and men's estimated earned income.

Measuring the HPI-1 and HPI-2
The HPI-1 measures deprivations in three basic dimensions of human development:
• A long and healthy life - vulnerability to death at a relatively early age, as measured by the probability at birth of not surviving to age 40.
• Knowledge - exclusion from the world of reading and communications, as measured by the adult literacy rate.
• A decent standard of living - lack of access to overall economic provisioning, as measured by the percentage of the population not using improved water sources and the percentage of children under five who are underweight.
The HPI-2 measures deprivations in the same dimensions as the HPI-1 and also captures social exclusion.
• Social exclusion - as measured by the rate of long-term unemployment (12 months or more).

WEBSITES

DEVELOPMENT ISSUES

World Watch Institute	www.worldwatch.org
New Internationalist Co-operative	www.newint.org
Bread for the World Institute	www.bread.org
One World	www.oneworld.org
Education Index	www.educationindex.com
Geography World	www.members.aol.com/bowermanb
World Interactive	http://www.worldinteractive.org
International Institution for Sustainable Development	http://iisd1.iisd.ca/
Earth Space Research Group	www.icess.ucsb.edu/esrg.html
Development Education Association	http://www.dea.org.uk
Oxfam	www.oxfam.org.uk/
21st century trust	www.21stcenturytrust.org
International Institute for Environment and Development	www.iied.org
Department for International Development	www.dfid.gov..uk
Royal Institute of International Affairs	www.riia.org

ENVIRONMENTAL ORGANISATIONS

World Resources Institute	www.wri.org
World Wide Fund for Nature	www.wwf-uk.org
The Earth Centre	www.earthcentre.uk.org
Forum for the Future	www.forumforthefuture.org.uk
Global Response	www.globalresponse.org
Earth Action	www.earthaction.org
Friends Of The Earth International	www.foe.org.uk
EcoNet	www.igc.org/igc/gateway/enindex.html
Envirolink	www.envirolink.org
International Society for Ecology & Culture	www.isec.org.uk
Greenpeace	www.greenpeace.org

UNITED NATIONS AGENCIES

United Nations	www.un.org
UN Development Programme	www.undp.org
UN Environment Programme	www.unep.org
UN High Commission for Refugees	www.unhcr.ch
UNICEF	www.unicef.org
UNICEF – for children	www.cyberschoolbus.org
UNICEF Voice of Youth Forum	www.unicef.org/voy
Food and Agricultural Organisation of the UN	www.fao.org

INTERNATIONAL ORGANISATIONS

The British Council	www.britcoun.org
The Commonwealth	www.thecommonwealth.org
Young Commonwealth	www.youngcommonwealth.org
Commonwealth Knowledge	www.commonwealthknowledge.net
European Parliament	www.europarl.eu.int/
Young European Movement	www.euromove.org.uk
North Atlantic Treaty Organisation (NATO)	www.nato.inl
Organisation for Economic Co-operation and Development (OECD)	www.oecd.org
NetAid	www.netaid.org

GLOBAL NEWS SERVICES

Worldwide News Sources	www.discover.co.uk
ForeignWire	www.foreignwire.com

REGIONAL NEWS

Africa News	www.africanews.org
Arabnet	www.arab.net
Latin America Bureau	www.lab.org.uk

ECONOMICS

New Economics Foundation	www.neweconomics.org
Heinz Centre	www.heinzctr.org
Jubilee 2000	www.jubilee2000uk.org

GOVERNANCE

International Institution for Democracy and Electoral Assistance	www.idea.int
International Relations and Security Network	www.isn.ethz.ch
Privacy International	www.privacy.org

HUMAN RIGHTS

Transparency International	www.transparency.org
Survival International	lwww.survival.org.uk
Amnesty International	www.amnesty.org.uk
World Organisation Against Torture	www.omet.org
National Peace Council	www.gn.apc.org/npc/

WOMEN'S ISSUES

Women and the Third World	women3rdworld.miningco.com
Feminist Activist Resources	www.igc.apc.org/women/feminist.html
Womankind	www.womankind.org.uk/

SETTLEMENTS

Centre for Environment and Human Settlement	http:www.eca.ac.uk/planning.cehs.htm
Eco-village Directory	http://www.ecovillages.org

POPULATION

UN Centre for Human Settlements-Habitat	www.undp.org/un/habitat
Population Concern	www.populationconcern.org.uk
Population Council	www.popcouncil.org
United Nations Fund for Population Activities	www.unfpa.org
UNDP Population Information (POPIN)	www.undp.org/popin/popin.htm

CONSUMERISM

Ethical Consumer	www.ethicalconsumer.org/index.htm
Enough, Anti-Consumerism Campaign	www.links2go.com/more/envirolink.org/issues/enough/in
Campaign for sustainable consumption	www.laslett.com/bananas.bananas.agoranet.be

YOUTH ACTION

YES! - Youth for Environmental Sanity	www.yesworld.org
Student Environmental Action Coalition	www.seac.org
YEE! - Youth and Environment Europe Web	www.netg.se/oppen/org/y/yee
UNICEF Voices of Youth	www.unicef.org/voy
YouthOrg UK	www.youth.org.uk
International Children's Action and Information Front	www.netgates.co.uk/icaif

Glossary

20:20 COMPACT	An agreement reached to get LEDC governments to allocate 20% of their budgets to basic social services and, in return, MEDC governments to allocate 20% of their ODA budgets to social services.
ABSOLUTE POVERTY	The lowest level of poverty where someone is living without the basic necessities of life.
AGENDA 21	Document produced at the UN Earth Summit in Rio de Janeiro in 1992. It is an action plan to achieve sustainable development in the 21st Century.
AID	The giving of money or goods to one country by another country or an organisation.
AIDS	Acquired Immunodeficiency Syndrome. A disease which destroys the body's natural immunity. It is spread through unprotected sex, blood transfusions or the sharing of syringes. There is no known cure.
APARTHEID	A system of governance where races are separated and treated differently.
BILATERAL AID	Aid given from one country directly to another.
BILLION	One thousand million: 1,000,000,000 (US billion).
BIODIVERSITY	The variety of plants and animals that exist in nature.
BIRTH RATE	The number of babies born per thousand people each year.
BRAIN DRAIN	The movement of highly educated and skilled people from poorer countries to richer countries.
BRACKISH	Slightly briny, salty, poor quality water
CASH CROPS	Crops such as tea, coffee, cocoa and tobacco, which are grown for export to make money.
CEDAW	Convention on the Elimination of All Forms of Discrimination Against Women
CHILD MORTALITY RATE	The number of deaths per thousand children under the age of five per year.
CIVIL WAR	An internal war within a country.
COLD WAR	The power struggle between the United States and the Soviet Union in the last half of the 20th century.
COLONIALISM	The practice of one country extending power and control over others.
COMMUNISM	A system of government which aims to establish a classless society and where the state owns all property and manages the economy.
CONSUMPTION	The purchase and use of goods and services.
CONVENTION	An agreement between governments
CORRUPTION	Using money or contacts for unfair personal gain.
COST-BENEFIT ANALYSIS	A study which looks at the full range of costs and benefits of a particular project.
DEATH RATE	The number of deaths per thousand people each year.
DEFORESTATION	Clearing forests of trees.
DEMOCRACY	A system of government where politicians are elected by the people through a secret vote.
DEMOGRAPHIC TRANSITION MODEL	A diagrammatic model showing changes in the birth and death rates of a population over time.
DEPENDENCY RATIO	The ratio between the economically and non-economically active members of a society.
DEVELOPED COUNTRIES	The richer, more industrialised nations of the world.
DEVELOPING COUNTRIES	The poorer, less industrialised nations of the world.
DEVELOPMENT	The processes of change, usually taken to mean industrialisation and economic growth.
EARTH SUMMIT	A international meeting held in Rio de Janeiro in 1992 for world leaders to discuss sustainable development.
ECO-TOURISM	A form of tourism which tries to minimise damage to local cultures or the environment.
EMERGENCY AID	Aid given in times of emergency. For example, after a natural disaster such as an earthquake or flood.
EMPOWER	To give someone the confidence and ability to do things.
ENVIRONMENT	The land all around us, the atmosphere, animals and plants.
EU	European Union. An economic and political association of European countries.
EXPORT	To sell goods or services abroad.
FAIR TRADE	A system of trade where the people who grow the crops used in a product are given a fair wage.
FAMILY PLANNING	Methods to control the number of children a woman has.
FDI	Foreign Direct Investment. Investment in a country by a corporation from another country
FERTILITY RATE	The average number of children born to each woman.
FINANCIAL CAPITAL	Everything that has a monetary value.
FIRST WORLD	An old term used to describe the richer countries of the world.
FREE TRADE	A form of trade where all taxes and quotas are removed.
G8	The Group of Eight. An association of the eight richest and most powerful countries in the world.
G77	The Group of Seventy-Seven. An association of many of the world's poorest countries.
GATT	General Agreement on Tariffs and Trade. An international agreement to reduce trade restrictions.
GDI	Gender Development Index. A measurement of the level of human development for women.
GDP	Gross Domestic Product. The total income generated in a country in one year.
GEM	Gender Empowerment Measure. A measurement of women's political and professional empowerment.
GENETIC MODIFICATION	The process by which a natural organism or product has its genetic make-up altered using modern biotechnology.
GLOBALISATION	The process by which goods, knowledge, ideas and people are exchanged between countries worldwide.
GNP	Gross National Product. The total economic value of a country's goods and services, including foreign earnings and investment, per year. The GNP per capita is the GNP figure divided by the population figure.
GOVERNANCE	The way in which a country is organised and managed, including its political and economic system.
GREEN ACCOUNTING	A system of accounting which counts the cost to the environment of different activities.
HDI	Human Development Index. A measure of well-being based on life expectancy, adult literacy, school enrollments and GNP per capita.
HDR	Human Development Report. A book covering different development themes each year, produced by the United Nations Development Programme.
HFI	Human Freedom Index. A measurement of levels of freedom in different countries around the world.
HIV	Human Immunodeficiency Virus. The virus which leads to AIDS.

HPI	Human Poverty Index. A basic measure of human poverty levels.
HUMAN CAPITAL	People and their skills or abilities.
HUMAN DEVELOPMENT	A process of widening people's choices so that they can live lives that they value.
HUMAN POVERTY	Deprivations in the most basic of human needs.
ILLITERACY	The state of being unable to read or write
IMF	International Monetary Fund. Set up to lend money to countries facing financial crisis.
IMPORT	To buy in goods or services from another country.
INCOME	The amount of money a person, corporation or country earns.
INDICATORS	Measurements which can be used to assess the state of things.
INDIGENOUS	Describes the original inhabitants of an area.
INDUSTRIALISATION	The process by which a country sets up industries.
INFANT MORTALITY RATE	The number of deaths per thousand of children under the age of one per year.
INTEREST RATE	The amount of money which must be paid back each month or year as part of a loan.
JUBILEE 2000	A coalition of groups campaigning for the cancellation of the debt of the world's poorest countries.
LEDC	Less Economically Developed Country. One of the poorer countries of the world.
LIFE EXPECTANCY	Number of years people are expected to live.
LITERACY RATE	% of adults in a nation who can read and write.
LONG TERM AID	Aid given over a number of years.
MALNUTRITION	Ill-health caused by an inadequate diet of quality food
MARGINALISATION	The process by which people are relegated to the fringes of society and made to seem unimportant
MATERNITY LEAVE	Time off work for women after they have given birth.
MEDC	More Economically Developed Country. One of the richer countries of the world.
MEGACITIES	Cities with a population of over 10 million people.
MICROCREDIT	Small scale loans, often with low interest rates.
MIGRATION	The voluntary or forced movement of people either within or between countries.
MULTILATERAL AID	Aid given by a number of different countries.
NAFTA	North American Free Trade Agreement
NATURAL INCREASE	The increase in population because of more births than deaths. It is calculated by subtracting the death rate from the birth rate.
NON-GOVERNMENTAL ORGANISATIONS	Charities and pressure groups, independent of governments and political parties.
ODA	Overseas Development Assistance or Aid. Money or goods given by a rich country to a poorer one.
OECD	Organisation for Economic Co-operation and Development, based in Paris.
ORGANIC FOOD	Food that has been produced without artificial chemicals.
OVER-POPULATION	A situation where the population of a certain area is too large for the local resources to support.
OVER-CONSUMPTION	Buying and using too many goods and services.
PATERNITY LEAVE	Time off work for a father after his partner has given birth.
POPULATION DENSITY	The number of people living in an area. It is calculated by dividing the total population by the total area.
POVERTY	Living on a very low income with few possessions.
POVERTY LINE	A measurement of basic levels of poverty
PRIMARY COMMODITIES	Crops and minerals which can be sold unprocessed.
PRIMARY HEALTH CARE	Basic health care often based in local clinics rather than in hospitals.
PUSH FACTORS	The factors which push people away from rural areas.
PULL FACTORS	The factors which attract people into urban areas.

RELATIVE POVERTY	Poverty which exists in comparison to wealth.
RENEWABLE RESOURCES	Natural resources which can be replaced or used again and again, like wind, water and solar energy.
RESOURCE	A part of the natural environment which can be used.
RURAL-URBAN MIGRATION	The movement of people away from the countryside into towns and cities.
SANITATION	The removal and treatment of waste, water, and sewage.
SAPs	Structural Adjustment Programmes. Policies introduced by the IMF and World Bank to help poor countries re-pay their debts by reducing social spending and increasing cash crops and exports.
SHANTY TOWNS	Unplanned urban settlements with few or no services and amenities.
SOCIAL SECURITY	Money and assistance given to people by the state.
SOCIAL SERVICES	Services, such as health care and education, provided by the state.
STANDARD OF LIVING	The conditions in which people live, including their housing, employment and social services.
SUBURBS	The outside regions of an urban area.
SUBURBANISATION	The process of people moving into suburbs
SUSTAINABLE DEVELOPMENT	"Meeting the needs of today without compromising the needs of tomorrow".
TARIFF	A charge made for bringing goods into a country
THIRD WORLD	An old term for describing the less economically developed nations of the world.
TIED AID	Aid which has to be spent on particular goods or services from the donor country.
TOBIN TAX	An idea to tax international money transactions.
TRADE	The exchange of goods and services between individuals, companies or countries.
TRADE BARRIERS	The taxes on the buying or selling of goods and services between countries.
TRADING BLOC	A group of countries which set trade policy together.
TRANSNATIONAL CORPORATION	Large company with offices or factories in several countries.
U5MR	Under 5 Mortality Rate. The number of children out of every thousand who die before they are five
UN	United Nations. An inter-governmental organisation that promotes world peace and fosters international co-operation.
UNDER POPULATION	Having more resources and facilities than there are people to use them per year.
UNDP	United Nations Development Programme. An organisation which produces the HDRs and which carries out development projects around the world.
UNEP	United Nations Environment Programme. An organisation which researches problems and proposes solutions to do with the environment.
UNFPA	United Nations Fund for Population Activities. The UN group that tries to slow population growth by promoting birth control techniques & family planning services.
UNICEF	United Nations Children's Fund. An organisation which works with disadvantaged children.
UNIVERSAL DECLARATION OF HUMAN RIGHTS	A document signed in 1948 by 150 countries which sets out the human rights of people worldwide.
UNSUSTAINABLE	A process or life-style which cannot be maintained
UN-TIED AID	Aid which can be spent on anything by the recipient.
URBANISATION	The process whereby an increasing proportion of people live in urban areas.
WHO	World Health Organisation. A part of the United Nations which deals with health issues.
WORLD BANK	A global bank which lends and gives LEDC governments money for long term development projects.
WTO	World Trade Organisation. An organisation created in 1995 to set global trade rules and promote free trade.

Acknowledgements

		Africa
ALGERIA	Mr. Karim Boubred Peace Child: Algeria,	
BENIN	Mr Raymond Gbedo M.S. Planete Terre-Benin	
CAMEROON	Mr. Ndjama Benjamin Solidarite et Prospective	
CAMEROON	Mr. Daniel Juwel Ngungoh Rescue Mission: Cameroon	
COMOROS	Ms. Sitti Fatouma Ahmed Espoir	
THE GAMBIA	Mr. Buramanding Kinteh Rescue Mission Gambia & Essau School	
GHANA	Ms. Fidelia Adomako-Mensah Members of Life-Link Friendship Schools	
GHANA	Mr. Edward Appiah - Brafoh Green Earth Organization	
GHANA	Mr. Charles Brown Friends of the Poor	
GHANA	Mr. Isaac Newton Kusi Ashanti Goldfields School	
LIBERIA	Mr. Richelieu M. Allison Voice of the Future	
MADAGASCAR	Ms. Bakolinirina Robertine Ravinala Group	
MOROCCO	Mr. Driss Guerraoni Le Forum des Jeunes Pour Le Millénaire	
NIGER	Hadjana Kadu Sani Nazarin Matassa Akano Aboulganiy, The Green Generation	
NIGERIA	Mr. Daniel Onyebuchi Eboh The Ebonite Foundation	
NIGERIA	Mr. Chris N. Ugwu Nigeria Society for the Improvement of Rural People (NSIRP) - "Youth For Development"	
SOUTH AFRICA	Ms. Yolandi-Eloise Realitivity	
SOUTH AFRICA	Ms. Anne Mearns The Wilger Veld and Youth Conservation Club	
TUNISIA	Mr Mustapha Couikha Youth Ending Hunger	
UGANDA	Mr. Mutyaba Andrew Rescue Mission: Uganda	
UGANDA	Mr. David Gonyiti Bulaago Youth Environment Project	
UGANDA	Ms. Mukasa Desire Ssaalongo St John Bosco Katende p/s	

		Asia
AFGHANISTAN	Ms. Zuhra Bahman Youth and Children Development Program	
INDIA	M. Rajayyan Ariyancode (Youth Wing of PADS)	
INDIA	Mr. Bremley Lyngoh C.I.S.S.D	
INDIA	Mr. Dhruv Malhotra Youth Led Action Network	
INDIA	Mrs Neera Mathur Maharaja Sawai Man Singh Vidyalaya	
INDIA	Mr. Pravin A. Mote Shrusti	
INDIA	Ms. Juhi Nagarkatti Jagaran	
INDIA	Ms. Anika Singh The Possibility Generation (TPG)	
INDIA	Mr. Samuel Talari Barath Peace-2	
INDONESIA	Ms. Anita Permatagari	
OMAN	Ms. Sara Al Asfoor Green Beans	
THE PHILIPPINES	Mr. Precy B Roma Peace Child Development Club	
NEPAL	Mr Ashish Suwal Paradise English Boarding School	
NEPAL	Ms. Urjana Shrestha Peacechild - Nepal (Eco-Nepal)	
NEPAL	Mr. Santa Rai, Ms. Julie Birnbaum, Mr. KanchiMaya Lama Yangrima School	
PAKISTAN	Zulfiqar Ali Human Rights Education Programme	
PAKISTAN	Mr. Masood-Ul-Haq Pakistan Environmental Lobbying Society	
SRI LANKA	Ms. Ermiza Tegal R.E.P.	
SRI LANKA	Mr. Mohamed Shukry Help For Youth	
VIETNAM	Ms. Vu Thuy Anh	

		America
ARGENTINA	Ms. María Eugenia Vicente Arbisu Nature	
ARGENTINA	Mr. Christian Javier Braga E.E.M.N. 2 O.E.A. - Carlos Spegazzini	
ARGENTINA	Ms. Pamela Castro	
ARGENTINA	Ms. Valeria Gilardone Pacto Familiar	
ARGENTINA	Mr. Francisco Gustavo Pazzarelli	
ARGENTINA	Ms. Vanesa Pressel Girasoles	
ARGENTINA	Ms. Natalia Ramos	
ARGENTINA	Ms. Bibiana Vilá Los Verdecitos (Profauna)	
BRAZIL	Ms. Roberta Márquez Benazzi Sharing The World	
ECUADOR	Ms. Stephanie Wilks Escuela Para Niñas Abraham Lincoln	
PERU	Ms. Carmen o Miguel Misión Rescate Planeta Tierra	
CANADA	Mrs. Susan Hawkins Rescue Mission: Canada	

BOSNIA-HERZEGOVINA	Ms. Azemira Delić-Muhurdarević	First Bosniak High School
CZECH REPUBLIC	Ms. Radmila Pavelková	Blue Stars
CZECH REPUBLIC	Ms. Blanka Tomančáková	Unesco Club Olomouc
FINLAND	Ms. Anja Kainu, Pirkko Koskela	Puolalanmäki Agenda 21 Group
MACEDONIA	Mr. Zuizanac Dragi	First Children's Embassy
POLAND	Ms. Maria Glowacka	Polish Ozone Group
SPAIN	Ms. Carmen Dolores Armas Hernández	C.P. Las Manchas
SPAIN	Mr. Manuel A. Fernández	Taller Educación Ambiental
RUSSIA	Mr. Gennady Nefedyov	Peace Child Krasnoyarsk
RUSSIA	Ms. Marina Trofimova	Physico-Technical Lyceum No 1
TURKEY	Ms.Birce Boğa	Rescue Mission: Turkey
UNITED KINGDOM	Mr. Tom Burke	Voice Of Plymouth Schools (VOPS)
UNITED KINGDOM	Ms.Venus A-Carew	Baha'i Peacemaker Club
UNITED KINGDOM	Ms. Joanna Carter, Deputy Head	Goonhaven Primary School
UNITED KINGDOM	Ms. Sarah Dorow (via Mr. Julian Cottenden)	Sandown High School, Isle of Wight, Life Link
UNITED KINGDOM	Mrs. Deb Hoskins	Millbrook School Rescue Mission Group
UNITED KINGDOM	Mrs. Diane Locke	Oaklands Primary School
UNITED KINGDOM	Mrs C E Martin	The Green Group, Fallibroome High School
UNITED KINGDOM	Mr J Robson	Kings Manor School
UNITED KINGDOM	Ms. Marielle Smith	Freman College
YUGOSLAVIA	Ms. Erika Papp	United Games Subotica

Europe

Book List

MARY BRADFORD
More questions and answers on the debt crisis
Christian Aid, London.

BUILDING AND SOCIAL HOUSING FOUNDATION
The City of Curitiba: Factors behind a success story
2000, Building and Social Housing Foundation.

MARTIN DREWY AND JUSTIN MACMULLAN
Questions and answers on the debt crisis
Christian Aid, London.

INGRID HANSON (ED)
The Debt Cutter's Handbook
1996, Jubilee 2000, London.

THE INTERNATIONAL SOCIETY FOR EDUCATIONAL INFORMATION, INC.
The Japan of Today
1989, The International Society for Educational Information, Inc., Tokyo.

MICHAEL KEATING
Agenda for Change. A plain language of version of Agenda 21 and the other Rio Agreements.
1993, Centre for Our Common Future, Geneva.

MOLLY O'MEARA
'How Mid-Sized Cities Can Avoid Strangulation' in World Watch, Vol. 11, NO. 5
1998, Washington.

BOB DIGBY AND OTHERS
It's a World Thing
2001, Oxford University Press

DAVID WAUGH
The New Wider World
1998, Thomas Nelson & Sons Ltd, Walton-on Thames.

WORLD BOOK INTERNATIONAL
The World Book Encyclopedia
1997, World Book Inc. Chicago.

UNITED NATIONS NON-GOVERNMENTAL LIAISON SERVICE
Economic and Social Development in the United Nations System. A Guide for NGOs
1999, United Nations Non-Governmental Liaison Service (NGLS), Tokyo & New York

UNITED NATIONS POPULATION FUND
The State of World Population 1999. 6 Billion: A Time for Choices
1999, United Nations Publications, New York.

INDEX

Grid Index - Geography

TOPIC AREA	THEMES	PAGE REFERENCE	EXAM BOARD REFERENCES
POPULATION	Global population distribution and change; Birth rate, death rate and natural increase; Demographic transition model; Dependency ratio; Emigration, Immigration and international migration; Population pyramids; Population management – family planning and education; Comparisons; Consequences of population growth; Differences between MEDCs and LEDCs	Population: pp30-31 Growing Trends pp32-33 Population Challenges pp34-35 What Are The Solutions?	AQA Syllabus A – 10.1 Population AQA Syllabus B – 12.1 Population growth and urbanisation AQA Syllabus C – 8.1 Managing Change in the Human Environment Edexcel A - Unit A2 (core): The human world (2.1-2.2) Edexcel B - Unit A1 (core): Providing for population change – Population dynamics (1.1-1.3) OCR Syllabus A – Unit 2 People and Places to Live – Population (a-c) OCR Syllabus C- Theme 4 (a) Wales Syllabus 1 2D Global Inequalities exist in the balance between population and resources (1)
SETTLEMENTS	Factors affecting settlements; Urban geography; Global pattern of urbanisation; Managing growth; Problems of urbanisation, including environmental, social and economic; Rural depopulation including push and pull factors; Shanty towns; MEDCs and LEDCs comparisons; Provision of services; Access to different types of housing	Settlements: pp36-37 A Changing World pp38-39 The Urban Challenge pp40-41 Are Sustainable Cities Possible?	AQA Syllabus A – 10.1 Population AQA Syllabus A – 10.2 Settlement AQA Syllabus B – 12.1 Population growth and urbanisation AQA Syllabus C – 8.1 Managing Change in the Human Environment Edexcel A – Unit C8 (option): Managing urban areas (8.2-8.3) Edexcel B – Unit A2 (core): Planning for change – Settlement (2.2-2.3) Edexcel short course – Unit 4 Managing urban areas (8.2-8.3) OCR Syllabus A – Unit 2 People and Places to Live – Settlement (a,c,d,e) OCR Syllabus B – Unit 3 People and place – Urban Rural Interaction (6-9), OCR Syllabus C- Theme 4 (d) OCR Short Course – Unit 2 People and Places to Live (a-e) Wales 1 Unit 2B – The Interdependent World – Economic and social change influence urban development (1,4)
ECONOMY AND INDUSTRY	Primary, secondary, tertiary and quaternary industries; Change in industry over time; Case studies; TNCs; Formal and Informal sectors; Employment patterns	Our Divided World: pp18-19 Contrasts In Experience Globalisation: pp42-43 The Problems pp44-45 The Solutions p46 Transnational Corporations	AQA Syllabus A – 10.4 Industry Edexcel A - Unit A3 (core): The economic world (3.1, 3.3) Edexcel B – Unit A2 (core): Planning for change – Employment (2.4) OCR Syllabus A – Unit 3 People and their Needs – Quality of Life (a-b); Economic Activities (d) OCR Syllabus B – Unit 4 People, Work and Development – Development, Trade and Aid (4-5) OCR Syllabus C- Theme 3 Economic Systems and Development (b,c) Wales 1 Unit 2A - The Interdependent World (4)

TOPIC AREA	THEMES	PAGE REFERENCE	EXAM BOARD REFERENCES
ENVIRONMENT AND RESOURCE USE	Environmental damage; Use of non-renewable resources; Sustainable resource management; Pollution; Renewable energy	Globalisation: pp48-49 Sustainable Development Consumption: pp26-27 How Long Can We Live Like This? Human Security: pp70-71 Other Knds of Security The Future: pp76-77 What Can You Do? pp78-79 Visions Of The Future	AQA Syllabus A – 10.5 Managing Resources AQA Syllabus C – 8.2 Managing the Physical Environment AQA Syllabus C – 8.3 Managing Economic Development Edexcel A – Unit B6 (option): Managing the environment (6.3) Edexcel B – Unit B4 (option): Use and abuse of the environment – Water (4.3) Edexcel short course – Unit 2 (6.3) OCR Syllabus A – Unit 4 People and the Environment – Resource Development and the Local Environments (c,d) OCR Syllabus B – Unit 1 Climate, The Environment and People - Eco-systems (7) OCR Syllabus C- Theme 2 Natural Hazards and People (c) OCR Syllabus C- Theme 5 Sustainable Development (a,b,c) OCR Short Course – Unit 3 Wales 1 Unit 1C The Fragile World (2) Wales 1 Unit 1D The Fragile World (1)
TOURISM	Impact on industry, the environment and the economy; Advantages and disadvantages; Causes of growth; Classification; Management; Case studies; Patterns of tourism; Eco-tourism	Globalisation: p47 Tourism	AQA Syllabus A – 10.5 Managing Resources AQA Syllabus C – 8.3 Managing Economic Development Edexcel A – Unit C7 (option): Managing tourism (7.1-7.3) Edexcel B- Unit C7 (option): Use and abuse of the environment – Recreation and Tourism (7.3) Edexcel short course – Unit 3 Managing Tourism (7.1-7.3) OCR Syllabus A – Unit 3 People and their needs – Economic Activities – (d) OCR Syllabus C- Theme 3 Economic Systems and Development (b) OCR Short Course – Unit 3 People and their Needs (d) Wales 1 Unit 1C - The Fragile World (2)
AGRICULTURE	Case studies of different farming systems; Agricultural problems and solutions; Commercial and subsistence farming		AQA Syllabus A – 10.3 Agriculture OCR Syllabus A – Unit 3 People and their Needs – Economic Activities (d)
DEVELOPMENT	Contrasts in development (e.g. literacy, health); Development indicators; Economic, environmental, social and political differences; Global trading system and solutions; Different types of aid; Case studies of aid; TNCs; Inequalities within countries; NGOs; Quality of life; Different forms of development; Relationship of aid and trade to development	Measuring Development: pp10-11 Measuring Development pp12-13 What Is Poverty? pp14-15 Other Indicators Of Development Our Divided World: pp16-17 Describing The Differences pp18-19 Contrasts In Experience pp20-21 Internal Differences Globalisation: pp42-43 The Problems pp44-45 The Solutions p46 Transnational Corporations p47 Tourism The Global Economy: pp50-51 The Politics Of Aid pp52-53 The Trading Game pp54-55 A Fate Worse Than Debt pp56-57 Trading together	AQA Syllabus A – 10.6 Development AQA Syllabus B – 12.2 Aid, investment and international development AQA Syllabus C – 8.3 Managing Economic Development OCR Syllabus B – Unit 4 People, Work and Development – Development, Trade and Aid (4-6) OCR Syllabus C- Theme 3 Economic Systems and Development (b,c) Wales 1Unit 2C – The Interdependent World (1,2) Wales Unit 2D – The Interdependent World (4)

Grid Index - Citizenship

CITIZENSHIP CURRICULUM KEY STAGE 4	COMMENTS
KNOWLEDGE SKILLS AND UNDERSTANDING	
KNOWLEDGE AND UNDERSTANDING ABOUT BECOMING INFORMED CITIZENS 1 Pupils should be taught about: a) the legal and human rights and responsibilities underpinning society and how they relate to citizens, including the role and operation of the criminal and civil justice systems.	Chapter 8 - Human Rights
b) the origins and implications of the diverse national, regional, religious and ethnic identities in the United Kingdom and the need for mutual respect and understanding	Pages 20-21 - Internal Differences
c) the work of parliament, the government and the courts in making and shaping the law	
d) the importance of playing an active part in democratic and electoral processes	Pages 60-61 - Good Governance Pages 76-77 - What You Can Do
e) how the economy functions including the role of business and financial services	
f) the opportunities for individuals and voluntary groups to bring about social change locally, nationally, in Europe and internationally	Pages 60-61 - Good Governance Pages 76-77 – What You Can Do Case Studies and Features – including Jubilee 2000, Fair Trade, Eco-labelling, No-Shop Day, Protests in Seattle.
g) the importance of a free press and the media's role in society, including the Internet, in providing information and affecting opinion	Pages 62-63 Corruption
h) the rights and responsibilities of consumers, employers and employees	Chapter 3 - Consumption Page 52 – Feature on Fair Trade Pages 56-57 - Trading Together Pages 74-75 – The United Nations
i) the United Kingdom's relations in Europe, including the European Union, and relations with the Commonwealth and the United Nations	
j) the wider issues and challenges of global interdependence and responsibility, including sustainable development and Local Agenda 21	All chapters Pages 48-49 – Sustainable Development
DEVELOPING SKILLS OF ENQUIRY AND COMMUNICATION 2 Pupils should be taught to: a) research a topical political, spiritual, moral, social or cultural issue, problem or event by analysing information from different sources, including ICT-based sources	Questions and Activities
b) express, justify and defend orally and in writing a personal opinion about such issues, problems or events	Questions and Activities
c) contribute to a group and exploratory class discussions and take part in formal debates	Questions and Activities
DEVELOPING SKILLS OF PARTICIPATION AND RESPONSIBLE ACTION 3 Pupils should be taught to : a) use their imagination to consider other people's experiences and be able to think about, express, explain and critically evaluate views that are not their own.	Questions and Activities
b) negotiate, decide and take part responsibly in school and community based activities.	
c) reflect on the process of participating	